Unlike Anything That Ever Floated

THE *MONITOR* AND *VIRGINIA* AND THE BATTLE OF HAMPTON ROADS, MARCH 8-9, 1862

by Dwight Sturtevant Hughes

EMERGING CIVIL WAR SERIES

Chris Mackowski, series editor
Chris Kolakowski, chief historian

The Emerging Civil War Series

offers compelling, easy-to-read overviews of some of the Civil War's most important battles and stories.

Recipient of the Army Historical Foundation's Lieutenant General Richard G. Trefry Award for contributions to the literature on the history of the U.S. Army

Also part of the Emerging Civil War Series:

For a complete list of titles in the Emerging Civil War Series, visit www.emergingcivilwar.com.

Unlike Anything That Ever Floated

THE *MONITOR* AND *VIRGINIA* AND THE BATTLE OF HAMPTON ROADS, MARCH 8-9, 1862

by Dwight Sturtevant Hughes

EMERGING CIVIL WAR SERIES

SB

Savas Beatie
California

First edition, first printing

ISBN-13 (paperback): 978-1-61121-525-0
ISBN-13 (ebook): 978-1-61121-526-7

Library of Congress Cataloging-in-Publication Data

Names: Hughes, Dwight Sturtevant, author.
Title: Unlike anything that ever floated : the Monitor and Virginia and the
    Battle of Hampton Roads, March 8-9, 1862 / by Dwight Sturtevant Hughes.
Other titles: Monitor and Virginia and the Battle of Hampton Roads, March
    8-9, 1862
Description: El Dorado Hills, CA : Savas Beatie LLC, [2020] | Summary: "The
    battle between the USS Monitor and the CSS Virginia (ex USS Merrimack)
    erupted in Hampton Roads, Virginia, Sunday, March 9, 1862. The day
    before, the Confederate ironclad ram had destroyed the wooden frigates
    USS Cumberland and USS Congress. This first engagement between ironclad
    steam warships represented naval, industrial, technological, and social
    revolutions during the American Civil War. The dramatic story unfolds
    through primary accounts of men who lived it."-- Provided by publisher.
Identifiers: LCCN 2020027492 | ISBN 9781611215250 (paperback) | ISBN
    9781611215267 (ebook)
Subjects: LCSH: Hampton Roads, Battle of, Va., 1862. | Monitor (Ironclad) |
    Virginia (Ironclad) | Virginia--History--Civil War, 1861-1865--Naval
    operations. | United States--History--Civil War, 1861-1865--Naval
    operations.
Classification: LCC E473.2 .H84 2020 | DDC 973.7/52--dc23
LC record available at https://lccn.loc.gov/2020027492

Published by
Savas Beatie LLC
989 Governor Drive, Suite 102
El Dorado Hills, California 95762
Phone: 916-941-6896
Email: sales@savasbeatie.com
Web: www.savasbeatie.com

Savas Beatie titles are available at special discounts for bulk purchases in the United States by corporations, institutions, and other organizations. For more details, please contact Special Sales, P.O. Box 4527, El Dorado Hills, CA 95762, or you may e-mail us at sales@savasbeatie.com, or visit our website at www.savasbeatie.com for additional information.

To the men and women of the United States Navy, past, present, and future guardians of our freedoms on the seas, and especially to my shipmates of a struggle more recent than the one depicted herein. We all are shipmates through the ages. Right full rudder. All engines ahead full.

Table of Contents

List of Maps

Maps by Edward Alexander

For the Emerging Civil War Series

Theodore P. Savas, *publisher*
Chris Mackowski, *series editor*
Christopher Kolakowski, *chief historian*
Sarah Keeney, *editorial consultant*
Kristopher D. White, *co-founding editor*

Publication supervision by Chris Mackowski
Design and layout by Savannah Rose

List of Diagrams

Diagrams by J.M. Caiella

Acknowledgments

I would like to thank Emerging Civil War editor-in-chief Chris Mackowski for his unwavering support, wise counsel, and notable patience as I worked through this manuscript, and to Chris Kolakowski, historian extraordinary, for the foreword. A hardy salute also to the whole gang at Emerging Civil War—a dedicated, talented group of public historians—for your warm friendship and inspiration. You have provided a home port from which to sail forth into the dangerous waters of a new career and a labor of love.

I also must acknowledge the great folks at The Mariners' Museum and Park in Newport News, VA, home of The USS *Monitor* Center, for their warm welcome and invaluable assistance: Jenna Dill (Marketing & Communications Manager), Jay E. Moore, Ph.D (Librarian Archivist), Julie Murphy (Writer/Researcher/Administrative Assistant), Marc Marsocci (Director, Digital Services), Lisa Williams (Digital Services Coordinator), Will Hoffman (Director of Conservation), and others not mentioned. Thanks especially to Julie and Will for preparing Appendix C.

And finally, a special thank you to John Quarstein, Director Emeritus USS *Monitor* Center, speaker, expert, and well-known author, for filling in details and preparing the Afterword and Appendix B.

PHOTO CREDITS:
Alamy Stock Photo (asp); Edward Alexander (ea); J. M. Caiella (jmc); Library of Congress (loc); Mariners' Museum and Park (mmp); Minnesota Historical Society (mnhs); National Oceanic and Atmospheric Administration, Monitor Collection (noaa); Naval History and Heritage Command (nhhc); Public domain in the United States published before January 1, 1925 (pd-us-expired); U. S. National Archives and Records Administration (nara); Wikimedia Commons: Creative Commons Attribution-Share Alike 3.0 Unported, https://creativecommons.org/licenses/by-sa/3.0/deed.en (wcca); Wikimedia Commons Public Domain (wcpd). Chris Heisey proved the background image on pages vi-ix and xviii-xix.

What's In A Name?

The infamous Rebel ironclad at Hampton Roads had two names and one of those names had two common spellings. She was officially commissioned the CSS *Virginia* when completed. However, most Northerners and many Southerners—including her own officers—continued to refer to her as *Merrimack* or *Merrimac* after the former U. S. steam frigate upon whose wooden hull the ironclad was constructed.

The USS *Merrimack* was named for the river that originates in New Hampshire and flows through the Massachusetts town of Merrimac, an older spelling of the river name without the final "k." The spellings are widely confused even in modern sources. The USS *Merrimack* was a famous ship, the pride of the U. S. Navy in the 1850s. Several of *Virginia's* officers had served in *Merrimack* prewar and all officers North and South knew of her.

Northerners preferred the original name while Southerners used it during the long conversion project and after commissioning as a matter of habit, practices that continued up to the present. The ironclad's official name was not widely used in contemporary writings although it probably would have caught on had she survived and served longer. The engagement in Hampton Roads is still incorrectly referenced—with memorable alliteration—as the Battle of the *Monitor* and the *Merrimack*.

This work employs official names in all textual references: *Virginia* for the Confederate ironclad and *Merrimack* only when discussing the former U. S. steam frigate. However, to preserve authenticity and narrative flow, quotes from participants have not been edited for spelling or usage (nor has "[sic]" been applied). Both spellings of the original name—*Merrimack* and *Merrimac*—appear in these quotes referencing the Rebel ironclad, as is clear from context.

Ship names are rendered in *italics* to avoid confusion with namesakes, e.g., the ironclad *Virginia*

A monument to the sixteen lost crewmembers of the *Monitor* is in Arlington National Cemetery. The unidentified remains of two of those crewmen are buried there. (cm)

and the Commonwealth of Virginia. Because the sea was until recent history an exclusively male domain and a lonely one, seamen tend to anthropomorphize their vessels especially as female. Following tradition, the female pronoun is applied. Ship names are not preceded by the definite article except when necessary for clarity or when present in quotes. The prefixes USS for United States Ship and CSS for Confederate States Ship are applied for clarity, although there were no contemporary navy standards for them and they were used only sporadically.

Position titles in the U. S. and Confederate navies should not be confused with officer ranks. Both navies began the war with no officer rank above captain, equivalent to army colonel. There were no general officers, which in navy terminology, would be called "flag officers" authorized to fly a distinctive banner in their "flagship" leading a fleet.

The U. S. Navy had never deployed large fleets and therefore did not need flag officers to command them. A senior captain assigned to command a squadron of a few warships used the title of flag officer or commodore. Later in 1862, both expanding navies established new flag officer ranks of admiral, which exist to this day.

The commanding officer of a commissioned warship carried the title and was addressed as captain regardless of rank. Ranked captains commanded the largest vessels but ranked commanders and senior lieutenants also commanded powerful ships. Small auxiliary vessels could be commanded by sailing masters, a warrant officer rank. A warship's second in command carried the title of executive officer. He usually was a lieutenant in rank.

The numbers of warships, guns and men noted below are approximate. Actual numbers varied in time and circumstance.

$\mathcal{F}$oreword

BY CHRISTOPHER KOLAKOWSKI

Visitors to Vienna, Austria, often pass by a large obelisk on the city's eastern side. The pole stretches high into the sky, its profile broken by the protruding silhouettes of ships' hulls. Those who approach see the inscription *Fighting Bravely at Heligoland/Triumphing Gloriously at Lissa/ He won Deathless Fame for/Himself and Austria's Sea Power*. This memorial to Admiral Wilhelm von Tegetthoff in many ways is the largest legacy to the ironclad warfare inaugurated by the clash of USS *Monitor* and CSS *Virginia* on March 8-9, 1862.

Monitor and *Virginia* were not the first ironclad warships built. Navies around the world had used iron in sailing ships and floating batteries for several centuries before the battle of Hampton Roads. Iron-hulled seagoing ships only became practicable after the perfection of steam propulsion in the middle of the nineteenth century. In 1859 the French Navy debuted the first true ironclad warship, *La Gloire*. A year later the British launched HMS *Warrior*, a faster and better-armed improvement on *La Gloire*. Both ships resembled wooden steamships, but featured iron hulls and watertight compartments belowdecks — elements now commonplace on modern warships. Neither vessel ever saw combat.

After the battle of Hampton Roads, the second-greatest battle of ironclads during the Civil War was the battle of Mobile Bay on August 5, 1864. A Union fleet of 18 ships under Vice Admiral David G. Farragut passed the narrow channel under Fort Morgan, losing one ship to an underwater mine. Confronted by the Confederate ironclad CSS *Tennessee*, Farragut drove her off in a short and sharp battle. *Tennessee* attacked again, starting

Admiral Wilhelm von Tegetthoff monument, Vienna, Austria. (asp)

At the Battle of Mobile Bay, August 5, 1864, Adm. Franklin Buchanan in the ironclad CSS *Tennessee* (center foreground) is surrounded and battered into submission by Adm. David G. Farragut's squadron. The gunboat USS *Ossipee* is about to ram *Tennessee*. Double-turreted monitors USS *Winnebago* (left) and USS *Chickasaw* (right) caused much damage with their 11-inch Dahlgrens. Farragut's flagship, USS *Hartford*, is center right. (nhhc)

an hour-long melee with the Union fleet. Both sides maneuvered to ram each other, with the faster Union ships striking more often. Meanwhile the heavy guns of ironclads *Manhattan* and *Chickasaw*, firing at point-blank range, did crippling damage to *Tennessee*. About 10:00 a.m., the Confederate ship struck her colors.

Meanwhile, European navies assessed American designs. They found the *Monitor*-class ships lacking in freeboard, which was essential for true oceangoing fleets. European naval architects instead sought to balance the sea-keeping capabilities of steamships while preserving the strength and protection of ironclad warships' hulls. Their resulting ironclads followed the lines of *Warrior* and *La Gloire* more than *Monitor* or *Manhattan*.

The American Civil War featured some of the best-known ironclad operations, but by no means the only ones that occurred at that time. Ironclads served on both sides of the 1864 Schleswig-Holstein War, but did not directly engage each other. The greatest ironclad battle in European waters, and the largest ironclad battle in history, occurred off the Adriatic island of Lissa (modern Vis) on July 20, 1866.

The former CSS *Stonewall* in Japan in the late 1860s. (nhhc)

Admiral von Tegetthoff attacked a larger Italian fleet that was protecting an invasion force. Outnumbered 7 ironclads to 12, von Tegetthoff boldly pierced the center of the Italian line and started a melee in which both sides maneuvered to ram. At the battle's climax, von Tegetthoff's flagship struck the Italian flagship, sinking her within minutes and causing the Italian fleet to retreat. The Austrian victory at Lissa broke Italian naval power in the Adriatic, and was one of the few bright spots for Austria that year.

Modern ironclads also spread to Asia when the Imperial Japanese Navy purchased the ram CSS *Stonewall* in 1865 and renamed her *Kosetsu*, later *Azuma*. This ship saw action around Japan in the various wars resulting from the Meiji Restoration, including helping end the Satsuma Rebellion. *Azuma* thus helped Japan keep pace technologically with Western navies, and influenced future Japanese warship design.

Hampton Roads, Mobile Bay, and Lissa all seemed to teach the same lessons. First, heavy shell was needed to penetrate enemy armor. Secondly, turrets proved their usefulness in all-around firing, but hull-mounted guns had their place in combat. Lastly, ramming had been a major part of the tactics of each engagement. These three basic assumptions governed naval architecture into the twentieth century.

Throughout the remainder of the nineteenth century, ship designers sought to balance these three imperatives for armament with the need to develop true oceangoing iron ships. It was a period of rapid progress, the greatest technological change in naval warfare until

The USS *Iowa* (BB-4) was a pre-dreadnought battleship commissioned in June 1897. She mounted four 12-inch guns firing an 850-pound shell from two turrets, eight 8-inch and six 4-inch guns in the secondary battery, and two 14-inch torpedo tubes. An improved steel armored belt 14 inches thick girded the central portion of the hull, protecting magazines and propulsion machinery. *Iowa* served through the First World War. Note the ram-equipped bow. (nhhc)

The USS *Olympia* (C-6) was a 344'-long protected cruiser that saw service from her commissioning in 1895 until 1922. She was the flagship of Commodore George Dewey at the Battle of Manila Bay (1898) during the Spanish American War, where her 8-inch guns devastated the enemy fleet. *Olympia* has been restored to her 1898 configuration as a museum ship in Philadelphia (part of the Independence Seaport Museum) and National Historic Landmark. She is the oldest steel American warship still afloat. (nhhc)

the introduction of the aircraft carrier. Navies around the world experimented with various designs to try and find the perfect harmony between elements. At the same time, breechloaders replaced muzzle-loading guns and steel began to supplant iron in hulls and armor.

Also during this period navies diversified, developing various types and sizes of ships for different missions. Whereas in 1864 Farragut had three types of ships under his command, by 1904 commanders would often have four or five types under command. Battleships were the heavyweights and main element of the battle line, while faster and lighter cruisers (divided further into heavy and light) ranged as scouts and administered sharp stings with their guns. Torpedo boats, later known as destroyers, were lightest and fastest of all, and took on the most specialized tasks. Colliers and supply ships also kept the fleet replenished and at sea for longer cruises.

The best examples of this period's designs occurred in the late 1880s and early 1890s. In the United States, the first battleships came about, namely USS *Indiana*, *Massachusetts*, *Oregon*, *Iowa*, and *Kentucky*. Heavy cruisers also appeared on the scene, including USS *Maine*, USS *Olympia*, and USS *New York*. In Britain, the battleships HMS *Victoria* and HMS *Camperdown*, commissioned in 1887 and 1889 respectively, typified how designers sought to balance armament, power, and armor. The collision of the two ships on June 22, 1893, when *Camperdown's* bow tore a giant hole into *Victoria* and caused her to rapidly sink, seemed to only confirm the ram's continued value.

War with Spain in 1898 proved a turning point in the history of iron navies. On May 1, 1898, Commodore George Dewey led a U.S. fleet into Manila Bay and in a few hours smashed a Spanish squadron. The following July 3, another U.S. fleet under William Sampson did the same thing to the Spanish fleet in the Caribbean off Santiago, Cuba. Firepower decided these engagements, with neither side closing to a range where ramming was possible.

The last great battle between iron navies occurred in Asian waters, at the battle of Tsushima in 1905. After many skirmishes in the Yellow Sea near Port Arthur, Japanese and Russian battle fleets met in the Tsushima Strait between Korea and Japan on May 27, 1905. As the fleets approached from opposite directions, Japanese Admiral Togo Heihachiro chose not to close the range and ram, instead opting to depend on his ships' maneuverability and gunnery. The result was one of the most lopsided naval victories in history, with over two-thirds of the Russian fleet sunk or captured against Japanese losses of 3 torpedo boats and 617 men.

Shortly afterward, navies around the world started seeking to decide engagements by firepower and at longer range than previously fought. This tactic required a battleship that would feature more big guns in turrets, with weight devoted to armor and without a heavy ramming bow. The result was the 1906 HMS *Dreadnought*, which changed naval warfare forever.

After nearly a half century, the era begun by the battle of Hampton Roads was over.

The Russian battleship *Orel* was damaged and captured by the Japanese in the Battle of Tsushima, 28 May 1905. The muzzle of this 12-inch gun was blown to the starboard side of the bridge and lodged in a signal locker. A Japanese sailor stands guard. (nhhc)

HMS *Dreadnought* was the next revolution in naval power, giving her name to an entire generation of battleships. She was armed with a uniform main battery of ten long-range 12-inch guns and powered for the first time by steam turbines. *Dreadnought's* launch fueled the naval arms race leading to the First World War. (nhhc)

"One may disagree with the phrasing of various historians on both sides . . . but no American can cease to wonder at the fortitude and daring of those other Americans who fought to the death in those hastily improvised crafts, bearing the brunt not only of battle, but of a strange and terrible experiment. It is not an argument that this book offers, but a saga of heroes, an illumination of qualities which have made our history in times of crisis."

— From the Introduction to *The Monitor and the Merrimac: Both Sides of The Story, Told by Lieut. J.L. Worden, U.S.N., Lieut. Greene, U.S.N. of the Monitor and H. Ashton Ramsay, C.S.N., Chief Engineer of the Merrimac (New York: 1912)*

Prologue

On the afternoon of March 9, 1862, Assistant Secretary of the United States Navy Gustavus Fox stood on the deck of a mighty warship watching the USS *Monitor* approach. "As we ran along side," wrote *Monitor's* Lt. Samuel Greene to his parents, "Secretary Fox hailed us, and told us we had fought the greatest naval battle on record and behaved as gallantly as men could. He saw the whole fight. I felt proud and happy then Mother, and felt fully repaid for all I had suffered."

Surviving sailors from the sunken USS *Cumberland* and the immolated USS *Congress* watched from shore. Seaman Frederick Curtis: "Our joy knew no bounds. All on shore cheered the brave little '*Monitor*' until they were hoarse, and many hugged one another for joy."

Across Hampton Roads, the CSS *Virginia* steamed up the Elizabeth River. "She received a tremendous ovation from the crowds that lined the shores, while hundreds of small boats, gay with flags and bunting, converted our course into a triumphal procession," recalled *Virginia's* Chief Engineer Ashton Ramsay. Thus ended the monumental first contest between ironclad warships.

The day before, *Virginia* had engaged both *Cumberland* and *Congress*. Union Fireman Joseph McDonald: "That great black thing, different from any vessel ever seen before, poked her nose around Sewell's Point and came directly for the two ships. . . . My, didn't orders ring out sharp, and men jump lively!"

According to one Confederate witness, this "huge, unwieldly make-shift" craft steamed out on that beautiful morning "officered with the very cream of the old navy, and manned by as gallant a crew as ever fought in a good cause—Southern born almost to a man. . . ." She was "freighted down to the very guards with the tearful prayers and hopes of a whole people. . . ." *Virginia's* Lt. John Eggleston: "The drum and fife are sounding the call to quarters. We go quietly to our stations, cast loose the guns, and stand ready for the next act in the drama."

The USS *Cumberland* "was a splendid type of the frigate of the old times, with her towering masts, long yards, and neat man-of-war appearance," wrote her executive officer, Lt. Thomas Selfridge. The crew "stood at their guns for the last time, cool, grim, silent and determined. . . . For what was known at that time of the relative merits of iron-clads and wooden ships?"

Nearby on *Congress,* Frederick Curtis manned his gun while the Rebel ram loomed closer. "Every eye on the vessel was on her. Not a word was spoken, and the silence that prevailed was awful. The time seemed hours before she reached us." Lieutenant Eggleston observed *Congress* through a *Virginia* gun port. "Suddenly there leaped from her sides the flash of thirty-five guns, and as many shot and shell were hurled against our armor only to be thrown from it high into the air."

"The action soon became general," reported Confederate Flag Officer Franklin Buchanan. "The *Cumberland, Congress,* gunboats and shore batteries concentrating upon us their heavy fire, which was returned with great spirit and determination."

Virginia rammed *Cumberland.* Lieutenant Robert Minor passed along *Virginia's* gundeck waving his cap, calling out, "We've sunk the *Cumberland.*" At his aft pivot gun, Lt. John Wood recalled: "The *Cumberland* continued the fight, though our ram had opened her side wide enough to drive in a horse and cart."

"Events followed too fast to record them," continued *Cumberland's* Lieutenant Selfridge. The dead were thrown over the side, wounded carried below. "No one flinched, but went on loading and firing, taking the place of some comrade, killed or wounded, as they had been told to do. But the carnage was something awful; great splinters, torn from the side, wounded more men than the shell."

Observers thronged the shore, among them Confederate Brig. Gen. R. E. Colston. "After one or two lurches, [*Cumberland's*] hull disappeared beneath the water. Most of her brave crew went down with their ship, but not with their colors, for the Union flag still floated defiantly from the masts."

Virginia turned toward *Congress*. "The lofty frigate, towering above the water, now offered an easy target," noted General Colston. "Projectiles hurled at the [*Virginia*] glanced harmlessly from her iron-covered roof, while her rifled guns raked the *Congress* from end to end. . . . The latter replied gallantly. . . . [H]er decks were reeking with slaughter."

"We raked her fore and aft with hot shot and shell, till out of pity we stopped without waiting for orders," wrote Lieutenant Eggleston. Flames crept up the rigging as dusk descended, recalled General Colston. "Every mast, spar, and rope glittered against the dark sky in dazzling lines of fire." Upon the hull's black surface, "each port-hole seemed the mouth of a fiery furnace."

That night, the USS *Monitor* steamed into Hampton Roads prepared for battle, but not all were sanguine about the results. "An atmosphere of gloom pervaded the fleet," wrote *Monitor's* Lieutenant Greene, "and the pygmy aspect of the new-comer did not inspire confidence among those who had witnessed the destruction of the day before." With the dawn, the ironclads sallied forth to meet in the middle of the Roads.

President Lincoln called an emergency cabinet meeting in the White House. That Sunday morning "was as gloomy as any that Washington had experienced since the beginning of the war," wrote a senior treasury official. "There was no excitement, but all seemed to be overwhelmed with despondency and vague apprehension."

Secretary of War Edwin Stanton feared the Rebel ram would destroy every Union naval vessel and then "come up the Potomac and disperse congress, destroy the Capitol and public buildings, or she might go to New York and Boston and destroy those cities. . . ." No Union warship, even *Monitor*, could stop her.

Meanwhile, aboard the Union ironclad, Paymaster William F. Keeler recalled: "We were enclosed in what we supposed to be an impenetrable armour—we knew that a powerful foe was about to meet us—ours was an untried experiment & our enemy's first fire might make it a coffin for us all. . . . The suspense was awful as we waited in the dim light expecting every moment to hear the crash of our enemy's shot."

The combatants circled awkwardly in what would appear to a modern observer as slow motion. Guns bellowed as fast as they could be served. Rounds screamed, clanged, boomed, and splashed all around. "The [*Virginia*] could not sink us if we let her pound us for a month," announced *Monitor's* commanding officer, Lt. John Worden after a few thunderous hits. "The men cheered; the knowledge put new life into all."

"We. . .were often within a ship's length [of *Monitor*]," reported *Virginia's* Lt. Catesby Jones. "Once while passing we fired a broadside at her only a few yards distant. She and her turret appeared to be under perfect control. Her light draft enabled her to move about us at pleasure."

"Five times during the engagement we touched each other," wrote Lieutenant Greene, "and each time I fired a gun at [*Virginia*], and I will vouch the 168 lbs. penetrated her sides. . . . The shot, shell, grape, canister, musket and rifle balls flew about us in every direction, but did us no damage. Our Tower was struck several times, and though the noise was pretty loud, it did not affect us any."

While *Virginia's* gundeck was all "bustle, smoke, grimy figures, and stern commands," recalled Engineer Ramsay, "down in the engine and boiler rooms the sixteen furnaces were belching out fire and smoke." Firemen toiled before the flames "like so many gladiators" shoveling and stirring coal, intensifying combustion and heat.

"The noise of the cracking, roaring fires, escaping steam, and the loud and labored pulsations of the engines, together with the roar of battle above and the thud and vibration of the huge masses of iron which were hurled against us produced a scene and sound to be compared only with the poet's picture of the lower regions."

Lieutenant Wood: "Again [*Monitor*] came up on our quarter, her bow against our side, and at this distance fired twice." Both shots struck halfway up the shield near the aft pivot gun, humping the entire iron and wood construction inward two or three inches. "All the crews of the after guns were knocked over by the concussion, and bled from the nose or ears. Another shot at the same place would have penetrated."

As the sun sank and the tide turned, the iron combatants finally separated, returning to their

THE LOSS OF THE USS MONITOR

In the age old battle of man against the sea, the *USS Monitor*, en route to Beaufort, North Carolina under tow by the *USS Rhode Island*, foundered in a gale sixteen miles off the coast of Cape Hatteras at approximately 1:30 a.m. on New Year's Eve 1862.

"We had left behind us, one more treasure added to the priceless store which the Ocean so jealously hides. The *Cumberland* and *Congress* went first; the little boat that avenged their loss has followed; in both noble souls have gone down. Their names are for history; and as long as we remain a people, so long will the work of the *Monitor* be remembered, and her story told to our children's children."

Greenville M. Weeks, Surgeon *USS Monitor*

respective sides. *Monitor's* Lieutenant Greene reflected on the experience for both sides: "Every bone in my body ached, my limbs and joints were so sore that I could not stand. My nerves and muscles twitched as though electric shocks were continually passing through them and my head ached as if it would burst."

How did this revolutionary engagement come about? What strategies and happenstance led to this moment? How were these metal monsters conceived, designed, constructed, and fought? Who won? What were the consequences for the struggle on both sides, and for the future of naval warfare?

The story of the *Monitor* would come to an end less than a year after her first combat. On New Year's Eve 1862, she foundered in a gale off Cape Hatteras, North Carolina. A monument to her sinking stands near the Graveyard of the Atlantic Museum in the village of Hatteras. "[A]s long as we remain a people, so long will the work of the *Monitor* be remembered, and her story told to our children's children," said ship's surgeon Greenville M. Weeks, quoted on the monument. The flip side memorializes "Maritime Casualties of the American Civil War." The site of the *Monitor's* sinking, some sixteen miles offshore, is now a national marine sanctuary.
(cm)

Prepare for Serious Work

CHAPTER ONE
MARCH 6 – 8, 1862

Thursday, March 6, 1862: The revolutionary—and rather bizarre—ironclad USS *Monitor* steamed out of New York harbor towed by the steam tug *Seth Low* and escorted by gunboats *Currituck* and *Sachem*. "4 o'clock P.M. We have just parted with our pilot & may consider ourselves at sea," wrote William F. Keeler to his wife Anna. "We have a fine westerly wind, a smooth sea & as fair a sky as we could expect. . . ."

Keeler, a forty-year-old senior partner in an Illinois ironworks manufacturing steam engines, left family and career to proudly join the United States Volunteer Navy as paymaster. His only maritime experience had been a passage to the California gold fields in 1849, then to China and home via the Cape of Good Hope. Excepting the captain, Keeler was the oldest officer aboard.

The paymaster managed provisions, clothing, stationery, and "small stores" such as tobacco, soap, candles, thread, buttons, needles, jack knives, "all the thousand & one things a Sailor will stand in need of" besides ship accounts and payroll. Letters to Anna recount his adventures from this first experience in *Monitor* to the last 10 months later when he barely escaped as she sank beneath him amidst monstrous waves and gale-force winds.

But on this day, the little vessel—173 feet long, 41.5 feet in beam—was much more buoyant than Keeler anticipated. Only a bit of water sloshed across the flat expanse of deck, which rested barely a foot and a half above the surface. The deck, girded by a thick armored belt, was essentially an iron-plated wooden raft constituting the upper half of the structure, or upper hull.

Visitors to the USS *Monitor* Center, Mariners' Museum & Park, Newport News, Virginia can walk the deck of this full-scale *Monitor* replica. (mmp)

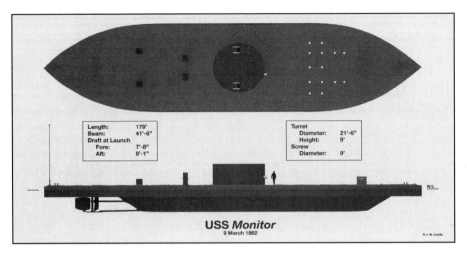

Length:	179'
Beam:	41'-6"
Draft at Launch	
Fore:	7'-8"
Aft:	8'-1"

Turret	
Diameter:	21'-6"
Height:	9'
Screw	
Diameter:	9'

USS Monitor
9 March 1862

© J. M. Caiella

Deck and profile views of Monitor in her March 9, 1862, battle configuration. Graphic by J. M. Caiella. (jmc)

Beneath the raft hung the lower hull, a flat-bottomed cradle constructed entirely of bolted and riveted iron plate and angle iron, giving *Monitor* a draft of 10.5 feet. The overhanging armored belt shielded the lower hull, anchor housing, and propeller from shot, shell, and ramming. The two hulls were joined by stanchions, brackets, and rivets with a watertight seal that proved problematic and might have been one cause for *Monitor*'s eventual loss.

The cylindrical iron gun turret (also "tower" or "citadel")—21 feet in diameter, 9 feet tall—squatted in the middle of the deck encapsulating two huge 11-inch Dahlgren smoothbore cannons. A slab-sided iron pilothouse with narrow viewing slits protruded 4 feet above the deck at the bow 50 feet forward of the turret. Behind the turret sat two 6-foot boiler exhaust stacks and two 4-foot air intake stacks; the stacks were about 2 feet square and were removable for battle.

Sixty-five men were encased in the lower hull below the waterline. Deck hatchways were closed and secured to exclude water. The only safe and dry external vantage point was atop the turret, accessed via ladders from the berth deck below, up through gratings in the turret floor, and up again through hatches in the turret top. In port, another ladder on the turret side led down to the deck, but this was removed at sea and in combat.

To mid-nineteenth century mariners, this enclosed, cramped, artificial space—foreshadowing future submarines—was a radical departure from sailing and fighting on open decks and in the high rigging of a traditional man-of-war, and not a little frightening. But Keeler reassured his wife, "Your better half will be in no more danger from rebel compliments than if he was seated with you at home. There isn't danger enough to give us any glory. . . . Not a man is exposed in action, our boilers & our entire machinery are completely & effectually protected."

Monitor redefined the relationship between men and machines in war, challenging ancient concepts of honor and valor. These developments paralleled the transformative combat experience of soldiers who began the conflict standing up in open fields, manfully confronting the enemy face to face, but ended up burrowing into trenches and crouching behind elaborate fortifications. Technology advanced the defense over offense.

Monitor would become a cultural icon of American industrial strength and ingenuity; she embodied and popularized social and institutional as well as industrial revolutions. But beforehand, public opinion was decidedly ambivalent concerning this strange watercraft. "Not a whistle sounded to cheer us as we went out [of New York]," recalled one crewman. "Those we passed seemed to think it would be better to have played the funeral dirge than to give us the customary cheer."

The transition in one generation from timeless horse-drawn conveyance to huge, puffing locomotives had been breathtaking. On the water, tall warships had always inspired awe, but so far, they looked much the same even when driven by steam as well as sail. It was

An unnamed paddlewheel ocean tug nearly identical—103' long, 22' beam, 7' draft—to the USS *Seth Low*, which towed *Monitor* from New York to Hampton Roads. Driven by steam pistons, the "walking beam" towering above the ship oscillated up and down converting linear motion through crankshafts to rotating paddlewheels. This common arrangement was vulnerable to cannon fire. The tug is anchored at City Point, Virginia, main Union supply base on the James River later in the war. Note steam vessels and forest of masts in background. (loc)

William Frederick Keeler, Acting Assistant Paymaster and Clerk, USVN (1821-1886) wrote the most comprehensive and insightful personal account of life aboard *Monitor* (see Suggested Reading). His humble volunteer position required only writing and accounting skills, which as an experienced businessman, he had. Keeler also was technically knowledgeable from his steam-engine manufacturing business. (nhhc)

not clear where little *Monitor* fit in this transportation revolution. Was she even a ship or just an ironclad, two-gun battery that presumably floated and propelled itself?

"It is difficult to give an adequate impression in a few words," wrote a Vermont reporter. "[*Monitor*] is in fact unlike anything that ever floated on Neptune's bosom. The impression at a short distance is that of insignificance and harmlessness; but on standing upon its deck and looking upon it more closely, the impression is that of great power and invulnerability. The description of the Leviathan of the Scriptures very adequately expresses the feeling which this sea monster excites."

The vessel had a "most singular appearance" wrote Chief Engineer Alban C. Stimers to his father. From a half mile distant, she appeared to be sinking; the hull was not visible while the turret sat upon the water by itself. "People. . .said she looked like 'a wash-tub on a raft,' 'a cheese box on a plank,' 'a hat on a shingle' &c, &c."

Years later *Monitor*'s Captain John L. Worden recalled: "Here was an unknown, untried vessel, with all but a small portion of her below the waterline, her crew to live with the ocean beating over their heads—an iron coffin-like ship of which the gloomiest predictions were made, with her crew shut out from sunlight and the air above the sea, depending entirely on artificial means to supply the air they breathe. A failure of the machinery to do this would be almost certain death to her men."

Leaving New York, *Monitor* rushed down the coast toward Fort Monroe in Hampton Roads at the mouth of Chesapeake Bay in response to urgent intelligence that—any day now—the powerful Confederate ironclad ram, the CSS *Virginia*, would descend on defenseless wooden warships of the North Atlantic Blockading Squadron with devastating results.

Secretary of the Navy Gideon Welles ordered Captain Worden to exercise his men at the guns upon arrival, "and in all respects prepare for serious work." He was "not to go under fire of the enemies' batteries, except for some pressing emergency, until further orders from the Department." The secretary dispatched his assistant, Gustavus V. Fox, by land to meet *Monitor* at Fort Monroe. But as Welles noted: "Doubts were entertained and freely expressed whether the battery could perform the voyage."

That evening, Keeler mounted the turret to view the scene: "The moon is shining bright, the water smooth & everything seems favorable." Green lights glowed from the nearby gunboat while 400 feet ahead, the tug was "pulling lustily" at the big hawser. Several sets of white sails glistened farther off. "Not a sea has yet passed over our deck, it is as dry as when we left port. We had a merry company at the supper table." Captain Worden recounted amusing experiences as a midshipman.

Keeler described Worden as tall, thin, and quite effeminate looking, despite the long beard; he was pale and delicate, probably from long confinement. Keeler felt certain, however, that the new captain "will not hesitate to submit our ironsides to as severe a test as the most warlike could desire. He is a perfect gentleman in manner." The paymaster later credited Worden with a "noble kindness of heart & quiet unassuming manner." He "was nearly worshiped by us all."

A moderate breeze arose during the night, and by morning the vessel's motion was livelier. Keeler awoke in his elegantly appointed but dimly lit, closet-like cabin in the forward section of the ship. Just above his head, green water sloshed across the small, round glass window set in the main deck (a "deck light"), the only source of natural illumination.

Lieutenant Samuel D. Greene—executive officer and second in command—turned out of his bunk at 6:00 that Friday morning. Of the next three days, he later recalled: "I think I lived ten good years." Keeler noted this intimidating young officer with "black hair & eyes that look through a person" and did not doubt that all would obey him.

As the vessel wallowed, some, including Captain Worden and Surgeon Daniel C. Logue, complained of nausea and were laid out on the turret top for fresh air. The escorting gunboats were rolling heavily, occasionally dousing their gun muzzles in the waves and looking very uncomfortable, but *Monitor*'s open deck surface, low profile, and deep center of gravity brought relative stability.

"Her roll was very easy and slow, and not at all deep," reported Greene. "She pitched very little, and with no strain whatever. She is buoyant, but not very lively. The inconveniences we experienced can be easily remedied." He concluded, however, that *Monitor* was not a sea-going craft. She did not steer well; she did not have the steam power to make headway against wind or sea, and they were unable to work the guns with the gun ports—just 5 feet above water—closed and caulked.

By noon, a full gale blasted in from the northwest. "Now the top of every sea that breaks against our side

John Lorimer Worden, Lt., USN, (1818-1897) was a New Yorker who went to sea as a midshipman in 1834 becoming an experienced seaman in sail and steam. He would later command the monitor *Montauk* in action on the South Atlantic coast. Post war, Worden served as superintendent of the Naval Academy and commanded the European Squadron, retiring as rear admiral in 1886. (nhhc)

rolls unobstructed over our deck dashing & foaming at a terrible rate," wrote Keeler. "Our decks are constantly covered with a sea of foam pouring from one side to the other as the deck is inclined, while at short intervals a dense green sea rolls across with terrible force, breaking into foam at every obstruction. . . ."

Water blew through pilothouse eye slits, recorded Lieutenant Greene, knocking the helmsman from the wheel. It flowed under the base of the turret "like a waterfall" inundating sailors in their hammocks below. It squirted through the anchor chain port "in perfect floods," dripped around deck lights, and leaked through the berth deck hatch despite all efforts to prevent it.

It was, continued Keeler, "wet & very disagreeable below" in stuffy, lantern-lit spaces in unremitting motion.

USS *Monitor* Cross Section.
Graphic by J. M. Caiella. (jmc)

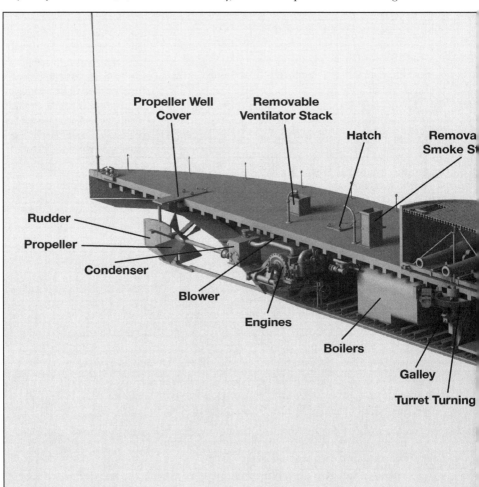

Propeller Well Cover

Removable Ventilator Stack

Hatch

Remova Smoke S

Rudder

Propeller

Condenser

Blower

Engines

Boilers

Galley

Turret Turning

"The accumulative weight [of water] seeming sufficient to bury us forever. The steady & monotonous clank, clank, of the engines assures us that they are still at work & the tug ahead is still pulling at the hawser, but as the day advances some anxious faces are seen."

About 4:00 p.m., Keeler gingerly descended the turret ladder to the berth deck where he encountered an engineer climbing up—pale, black, wet, staggering, gasping for breath and asking for brandy. Sailors hauled up other engineers and firemen, apparently lifeless. The door in the amidships bulkhead stood open, spewing steam, gas, and smoke, blinding and stifling everyone. This iron bulkhead supported the turret and separated engines, boilers, galley, and coal bunkers aft from crew and officers' quarters, magazine and shell room forward.

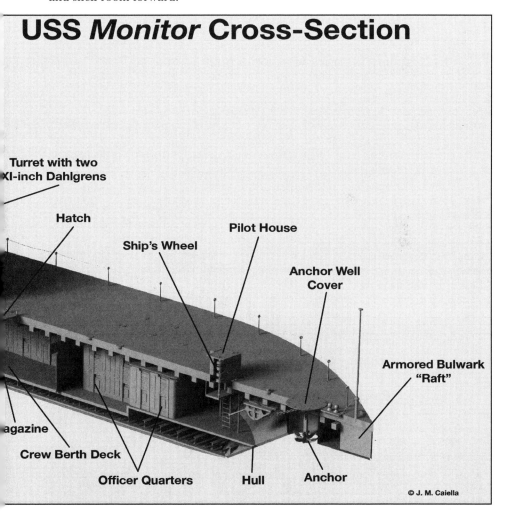

USS *Monitor* Cross-Section

Turret with two XI-inch Dahlgrens

Hatch

Ship's Wheel

Pilot House

Anchor Well Cover

Armored Bulwark "Raft"

Magazine

Crew Berth Deck

Officer Quarters

Hull

Anchor

© J. M. Caiella

Samuel Dana Greene, Sr., Lt., USN, (1839-1884) was a distant nephew of George Washington's most dependable general, Nathanael Greene, and son of Civil War General George S. Greene, who would notably defend the Union right flank at Culp's Hill during the Battle of Gettysburg. Samuel was among the first generation of U. S. Naval Academy-trained officers, graduating seventh in a class of twenty in June 1859. Post war, he served in and commanded several ships, and taught at the Naval Academy. Tragically, Commander Samuel Greene committed suicide on December 11, 1884 at the age of 45. (nhhc)

In this mockup at the *Monitor* Center, Lt. Greene enjoys a rare quiet moment reading in his cabin. He stores belongings in the drawers under and in the cupboards behind the bunk. At bottom right is a wash basin. (mmp)

Keeler hurried to shut the door but was told someone was still in there. Almost suffocating himself, the paymaster rushed in over heaps of coal and ashes followed by another crewman. They found a man lying insensible, dragged him out, closed the door, and lugged him up, but he was nearly gone.

Waves breaking over the short exhaust and intake stacks above the engine room rained torrents down on the machinery, bursting into steam in the boiler fires. Below the intake pipes, centrifugal forced-draft blowers provided the only source of fresh air for the engine room, the boilers, and the entire vessel interior.

The blowers, powered by leather drive belts from small auxiliary steam engines, pushed 7,000 cubic feet of air per minute. But the belts became soaked and started slipping, cutting off all draft.

Starved of oxygen, "the fires burned with a sickly blaze out of the ash pan doors, converting all the air in the engine and fire-rooms into carbonic-acid-gas, a few inhalations of which are sufficient to destroy animal life," wrote Engineer Stimers. Steam pressure plummeted; main engines stopped; the propeller ceased rotating; steam pumps would not operate. *Monitor* began to fill as she rolled.

Engineer Stimers ordered the men out but remained himself struggling with the blower belts until he began to get "very limber in the legs" and struggled up the ladder. "I managed to reach [the top] just as my strength gave out and I tumbled over upon the turret deck at full length."

In the best of circumstances, engine and boiler rooms were cramped and dusky domains of darkness and fire, intense heat and noise, smells of steel, steam, oil, coal, and sweat. The steam engine was a whirring, huffing, puffing, hissing, clanking, slick and oily, clamorous

monster with blindingly fast gears, shafts, and rods surrounded by imperfectly insulated scalding hot water and steam pipes, not to mention intense boiler fires. It was an encapsulated environment of impersonal, raw, self-generated power, and a dangerous and unpleasant place to work.

Lieutenant Greene never forgot the scene: "Our Engineers behaved like heroes every one of them." Greene assisted the evacuation, nearly suffocating himself. Sailors rigged an old piece of sail as an awning over the turret top for protection from wind and spray. "It was a sorry looking company which crowded the only habitable spot on our vessel," noted Keeler.

Water kept rising. Hand pumps lacked power to force water through hoses up and out the turret top, the only available point of discharge. Passing up heavy buckets proved impossible in the plunging vessel. "Then times looked rather blue I can assure you," wrote Greene. "What to do now we did not know. We had done all in our power and must let things take their own course." "We might have to 'give up the ship,'" reported Keeler.

They flew the ensign upside down from the turret as a universal signal of distress, but the escorting gunboats, rolling heavily themselves, could not approach. Worden hailed the tugboat and instructed her to steer directly for smoother water nearer shore. Finally, after five hours of struggle, the seas quieted; the vessel settled down.

By 8:00 p.m., engineers had mended blower belts, restoked boiler fires, and restarted main engines and blowers; pumps dewatered the engine room. With fresh air restored, the sick moved below. "My mechanical genius came in play," Keeler wrote to Anna. He took charge of the engines until morning when engineers were sufficiently recovered. But, "of course there was no sleep on board that night." Supper consisted of crackers, cheese, and water.

Monitor again encountered heavy seas while passing over a shoal around midnight. Water again inundated the blowers, which struggled and almost stopped. It was pitch black. Crewmen could not go out on the wave-battered, pitching deck. The tugboat—dead ahead at the other end of the towing hawser in the teeth of the wind—could not hear them call out. With no steam whistle, they could not signal their distress. They fought leaks all night. "We commenced to think then the *Monitor* would never see day light," recalled Greene.

Saturday morning came and the sea calmed but still washed across the deck. "It seemed singular to sit

Alban Crocker Stimers, Chief Engineer, USN, (1827-1876) superintended construction of the USS *Monitor* under direction of her inventor, Swedish engineer John Ericsson. Stimers continued to assist Ericsson with subsequent monitor-type ironclads including the highly successful *Passaic* class and the disastrous shallow-draft *Casco* class. (nhhc)

That monitors were not good sea-going craft is illustrated by a later *Passaic*-class monitor in moderate seas. The *Passaic's*, at 200 feet, were 20 feet longer than *Monitor*. Note the tall smokestack, pilothouse now atop the turret, and on deck, raised hatch comings and large curved ventilation intakes, all refinements on the original for keeping water out and letting air in. The turret is rotated with gun ports facing aft away from oncoming seas while crewmembers cling to lifelines. (nhhc)

in my room," wrote Keeler, "& hear the huge waves roll over my head & look up through the little deck light as the mass of water darkened the few straggling rays." Lieutenant Greene: "Nothing but the subsidence of the wind prevented her from being shipwrecked before she reached Hampton Roads."

Chief Engineer Stimers concluded that the vessel had not been properly caulked, and the air intake and smoke exhaust pipes were too short. However, "I consider the form and strength of the vessel equal to any weather I ever saw at sea." Sailors might be concerned about living under water, he continued, but "it is only the man who has studied the philosophical laws which govern floatation and stability who feels exactly comfortable in her during a gale of wind." The engineer would be proved tragically wrong on this point.

With her exhausted, dispirited crew, *Monitor* passed Cape Henry at the mouth of Chesapeake Bay at 4:00 p.m. on Saturday, March 8. The sudden transition from constant motion to relative stability in smoother waters kept head and stomach quivering for some time. "We imagined we heard heavy guns firing in the distance," reported Keeler. Captain Worden ordered the vessel stripped of her sea-rig, turret readied to rotate, and every preparation made for battle.

Halfway across the bay to Fortress Monroe on Old Point Comfort by 7:00 p.m., a harbor pilot boarded and informed them that the dreaded *Virginia* had been wreaking havoc. The USS *Cumberland* had sunk; the USS *Congress* had surrendered and was on fire.

"We did not credit it, at first," wrote Greene. "But as we approached Hampton Roads, we could see the fine old *Congress* burning brightly, and we knew then it must be so. Sadly indeed did we feel, to think those two fine old vessels had gone to their last homes, with so many of their brave crews. Our hearts were very full, and we vowed vengeance on the '*Merrimac*,' if it should ever be our lot to fall in with her."

Paymaster Keeler described plumes of smoke hanging over the land. Little black spots sprang into the air, paused for a moment, and then expanded into large white clouds. "As the darkness increased, the flashes of guns lit up the distant horizon & bursting shells flashed in the air."

Monitor pushed on with all haste, but, "how slow we seemed to move—the moments were hours." The engine clanked monotonously. There was no supper that evening. "As we neared the harbor the firing slackened & only an occasional gun lit up the darkness—vessels were leaving like a covey of frightened quails & their lights danced over the water in all directions."

This circa 1898 photo shows the engine room of the USS *Catskill*, a *Passaic*-class monitor, suggesting the confines aboard *Monitor*. The large wheel reverses the vessel's motion, ahead or astern, by redirecting steam through valves to opposite ends of the cylinders, thus reversing the motion of the pistons—after a full stop—and reversing shaft and propeller revolution, a slow process. Note large steam inlet pipe (vertical, top right) and exhaust pipe (horizontal, top left) and ladder up to main deck. (nhhc)

Fort Monroe loomed over this watery intersection. It served as the headquarters of Union Maj. Gen. John E. Wool, commander of the Department of Virginia. A young Union telegrapher, John Emmet O'Brien, watched from high in the citadel as *Monitor* approached through the dusk.

He had excitedly explored the great fortress with "all its mysteries of moat, casemates, ramparts, and water-battery; the big guns (Columbiads) mounted en barbette, some of which I could almost crawl into; the mortars with their piles of shot and shell, and the brick furnaces for heating hot shot, all on the ramparts. I wandered on the beach, listened to the sobbing of the tide, and saw the ships and steamers come and go, and, above all, admired the great sailing war-ships of the old navy."

On an earlier occasion—the telegraph line being down again—O'Brien had been dispatched by boat with a message for Brig. Gen. Joseph K. F. Mansfield commanding Camp Butler on Newport News Point. "As we steamed up through Hampton Roads to the broad mouth of the James River, I saw the Elizabeth River opening out behind Sewell's Point on our left (where the

One of the two ventilation blower intakes (short rectangular object in foreground) and the two collapsible boiler smokestacks are shown in this view of crewmembers on deck in the James River, July 1862. The sailor standing atop the turret holds a telescope, probably indicating that he is on watch. The cookstove is supported on bricks. (loc)

Merrimac was soon to come down); noticed the flagship *Minnesota*, with her graceful spars and long tiers of forty guns; the *Roanoke*; the frigate *Congress* and the sloop-of-war *Cumberland*, all peacefully at anchor in the Roads and seemingly invulnerable to any flotilla the enemy could improvise and send down either river against them."

Confederates had obstructed the Elizabeth River channel below Norfolk by driving piles and sinking hulks, leaving a narrow passageway. Rumors flowed via "contrabands" of something doing upriver at the Gosport Navy Yard. About March 1, 1862, recalled O'Brien, a German sailor had swum over with information of a "ball and bomb proof floating battery or ironclad."

This cutaway illustration of the ventilation blowers shows the troublesome drive belts, what engineers today would designate a single-point cascading failure, potentially catastrophic for the vessel. *Graphic by J. M. Caiella.* (jmc)

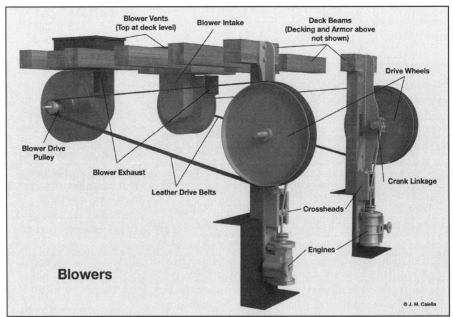

Blower Vents
(Top at deck level)

Blower Intake

Deck Beams
(Decking and Armor above not shown)

Drive Wheels

Blower Drive Pulley

Blower Exhaust

Leather Drive Belts

Crank Linkage

Crossheads

Engines

Blowers

© J. M. Caiella

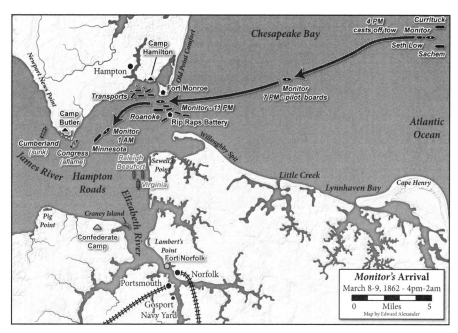

Monitor's Arrival
March 8-9, 1862 - 4pm-2am

0   Miles   5
Map by Edward Alexander

"We were, therefore, in daily expectation of the appearance of this unknown and untried monster. Daily our field glasses at Fort Monroe and Newport News swept Sewell's Point, Craney Island and the mouth of Elizabeth River."

On that Saturday evening, John O'Brien stood again on the ramparts watching *Congress* burn in the distance and fretting about his cousin who had been among *Cumberland*'s crew, when "I saw the dim outline of a queer, barge-like craft come into the Roads."

He hurried to headquarters where a fellow telegrapher tapped out a message from General Wool to General Mansfield at Camp Butler: "The ironclad Ericsson battery *Monitor* has arrived and will proceed to take care of the *Merrimac* in the morning." This missive also went to Secretary of War Edwin Stanton in Washington, but delayed by another telegraph line break, would not be received until the next afternoon.

Captain Worden brought *Monitor* to anchor off Fort Monroe at 9:00 p.m. near the powerful steam frigate USS *Roanoke*. He reported to Capt. John Marston, commander of *Roanoke* and acting commander of Union vessels in Hampton Roads. Marston had just received orders from Secretary Welles to send *Monitor* without delay up the Potomac to Washington, orders he wisely considered overcome by events. Similar instructions were sent to New York but arrived after *Monitor*'s departure.

MONITOR'S ARRIVAL— *Monitor* crosses Chesapeake Bay in the gathering dusk. On the horizon, shells burst in the air while the burning *Congress* competes with the setting sun. Dozens of merchant vessels flee in the opposite direction. Captain Worden reports to the flagship *Roanoke* and is ordered on into Hampton Roads to defend the grounded *Minnesota* near Newport News Point. *Virginia* and her consorts lay quietly at anchor under the guns of Sewell's Point.

Fort Monroe on Old Point Comfort in 1862 with the Hygeia Hotel in front and the fleet anchored in Chesapeake Bay at top right. Hampton Roads is to the left, the entrance channel in foreground. (loc)

The USS *Minnesota* had run hard aground off Newport News earlier in the day while pursuing the marauding *Virginia*. Assuming the Rebel ironclad would be back in the morning to finish the big frigate, Marston suggested that Worden stand by to defend her. "An atmosphere of gloom pervaded the fleet," recalled Lieutenant Greene, "and the pygmy aspect of the new-comer [*Monitor*] did not inspire confidence among those who had witnessed the destruction of the day before."

Civilian harbor pilots refused to guide *Monitor* up to Newport News with the unlikely excuse that they did not know the channel. The commander of the USS *Amanda* detailed his own navigator, Acting Master Samuel Howard; he would serve in *Monitor*'s pilothouse throughout the coming engagement.

The USS *Congress* blazed like a gigantic torch stuck in the mud where she had been pulverized

A 15-inch Rodman Columbiad, the "Lincoln Gun," on the ramparts of Fort Monroe with ships anchored in the background and a young soldier staring wistfully over the water. (loc)

The USS *Minnesota* was one of six nearly identical wooden screw frigates produced in the 1850s, the latest in naval technology. She was of a standard, sailing warship design with auxiliary steam engine. The first built was the USS *Merrimack*, and thus, the six are "sister ships" referred to collectively as *Merrimack*-class frigates. The USS *Roanoke*, also present in Hampton Roads, was another of the class. *Minnesota* was 275' long, 38.5' in beam, and 24' draft. She was rated for 646 men and 43 guns (8, 9, and 10 inch) although actual numbers would vary. (nhhc)

by *Virginia*. Illuminated by fire nearby, masts of the sunken USS *Cumberland* thrust above the quiet surface. *Monitor* steamed over to *Minnesota*, anchoring nearby at 11:30 p.m.

"Oh! you cannot imagine how our hearts rose within our breasts as the almost-too-joyous-to-be-real news reached us," wrote *Minnesota* Midshipman Charles S. Cotton. They had fought "against enormous odds" for six hours and had all night been struggling to get their ship off the bottom. "At 4:15 a.m. we all lay down as best we could to rest our weary limbs."

Lieutenant Greene boarded *Minnesota* and assured Capt. Gershom J. Van Brunt that they would do all in their power to protect her. As Greene returned to *Monitor* around 1:00 a.m., *Congress* blew up. "Certainly a grander sight was never seen, but it went straight to the marrow of our bones. . . . Not a word was said but deep did each man think and wish he was by the side of the *Merrimac*. Near us, too, at the bottom of the river, lay the *Cumberland*, with her silent crew of brave men, who died while fighting their guns to the water's edge."

Sink Before Surrender

CHAPTER TWO
MARCH 8, 1862 – MORNING

In the dawn of that tiresome Saturday, March 8, 1862—while *Monitor* wallowed in the wake of the Atlantic gale that almost doomed her—the CSS *Virginia* lay alongside the Gosport Shipyard quay on the west bank of the Elizabeth River across from Norfolk, Virginia, and just upriver from Hampton Roads. The storm passed in the night, leaving a cloudless morning, "calm and peaceful as a May day," recalled Midshipman Hardin B. Littlepage. The water's surface barely rippled in a soft breeze from the northeast.

Fifteen hundred men had labored for six months on this fearsome ironclad. She was a beehive of activity with mechanics and crew swarming to fit her for action. The wooden hull lay 263 feet long, 51 feet in beam, and 22 feet draft. On it a substantial casemate or armored shield had been constructed, 170 feet long and 12 high.

The casemate sides featured 4 inches of iron plate backed by 2 feet of pine and oak, angled at 36 degrees and slathered with tallow to deflect enemy shells. The deck on top—20 feet wide—was an open grating of iron bars admitting light and air. Hatches with pivoting iron shutters led by ladders to the gundeck below, which was 30 feet wide with 7 feet of headroom but only directly under the top deck.

Fourteen elliptical ports for a battery of ten guns pierced the casemate, three ports in each rounded end and four along each side. Seven-inch Brooke rifles on pivot mounts, one forward and one aft, could be aimed through either of the three end ports—directly ahead or astern, or at an angle to port or starboard.

This life-size mockup of *Virginia* at the *Monitor* Center shows the front of the casemate with workers installing gun port lids. Visitors can walk into the recreated casemate interior with mockup guns and equipment. (mmp)

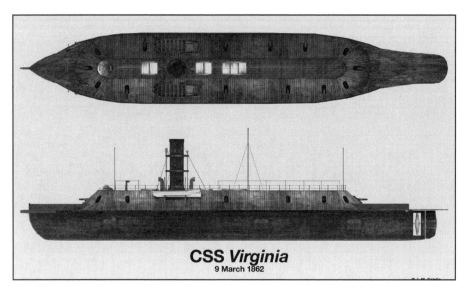

CSS *Virginia*
9 March 1862

Deck and profile views of *Virginia* in her March 8-9, 1862, battle configuration. *Graphic by J. M. Caiella.* (jmc)

Arrayed down each side were one 6.4-inch Brooke rifle and three 9-inch Dahlgren smoothbores. One Dahlgren on each side was equipped to fire round shot heated in a furnace below deck. The cannons were staggered along opposite broadsides to accommodate recoil and loading in the tight space under the sloping sides.

A small cast-iron, conical pilothouse with observation slits sat forward on the casemate while the big smokestack squatted in the middle. Armored decks fore and aft of the casemate lay just at the water's surface. "I could not see where she commenced or ended!" recalled one observer.

A stubby breakwater on the forward deck deflected water around the casemate and forward gun ports. Not visible under the prow and projecting forward two feet was a cast iron, wedge-shaped ram weighing 1,500 pounds (which would prove to be inadequately fastened).

Third Assistant Engineer Eugenius A. Jack thought *Virginia* looked like a sloping mansard house roof, but "the black mouthed guns peeping from the ports gave altogether different impressions and awakened hopes that ere long she would be belching fire and death from those ports, to the enemy and crashing into their wooden vessels with that formidable ram sending them to the bottom."

According to her surgeon, Dinwiddie B. Phillips, *Virginia* "bore some resemblance to a huge terrapin with a large round chimney about the middle of its back." She was not built for high winds or heavy seas and therefore could not operate outside the Virginia capes. "In fact she was designed from the first as a defense for the harbor of Norfolk, and for that alone."

Executive officer and second in command, Lt. Catesby ap R. Jones regarded the ironclad as incomplete as well as unseaworthy. There had been "many vexatious delays attending the fitting and equipment of the ship," mostly from want of skilled labor and lack of tools and appliances.

Virginia "was put up in the roughest way," wrote Confederate Army Capt. William Norris. She was "in every respect ill-proportioned and top-heavy; and what with her immense length and wretched engines. . .was little more manageable than a timber-raft. . . . She steered very badly, and both her rudder and screw were wholly unprotected." It would take 30 to 40 minutes just to turn her around, "and she never should have been found more than three hours sail from a machine shop."

The hull and engines came from the powerful steam frigate USS *Merrimack*, one of several warships burned and scuttled when Union forces abandoned Gosport to the Confederates in April 1861. Her engines were famously unreliable even before being immersed in the salty river for several weeks until the hulk could be raised and refurbished. Although *Virginia* presumably could do up to eight knots, most observers rated her between four and five knots.

Virginia was badly ventilated, very uncomfortable, and very unhealthy, continued Lieutenant Jones. "The crew, 320 in number, were obtained with great difficulty," mostly volunteers from various army regiments stationed about Norfolk. With 50 or 60 men in the hospital and others on the onboard sick list, the effective complement on this Saturday numbered about 250.

"There was a sprinkling of old man-of-war's men," recalled Lt. John R. Eggleston, "whose value at the time could not be overestimated." The rest "had never even seen a great gun like those they were soon to handle in a battle against the greatest of odds ever before successfully encountered."

With the ironclad mobbed by feverishly laboring mechanics, gun crews had been compelled to drill every day for two weeks at the old weapons onboard the venerable but decrepit frigate *United States* (renamed *Confederate States*), the only vessel Union forces did not bother to burn when they fled the facility. Their first and only practice behind *Virginia*'s guns would be in battle.

Catesby ap Roger Jones, Lt. CSN (1821-1877) was a Virginian matrilineally descended from William Byrd II, founder of Richmond, and Robert "King" Carter, making his mother a cousin of Robert E. Lee. His uncle Thomas Jones was a prominent naval officer who inspired characters in Herman Melville's *Moby Dick and White Jacket*. Catesby Jones became midshipman in 1836, attaining lieutenant before resigning. The "ap" in Jones's name is a Welsh patronymic meaning "son of." (nhhc)

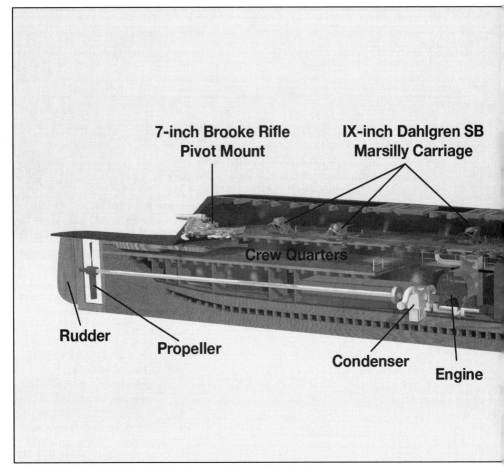

7-inch Brooke Rifle
Pivot Mount

IX-inch Dahlgren SB
Marsilly Carriage

Crew Quarters

Rudder

Propeller

Condenser

Engine

CSS *Virginia* Cross Section.
Graphic by J. M. Caiella. (jmc)

Two weeks earlier, on February 24, Secretary of the Navy Stephen R. Mallory appointed Capt. Franklin Buchanan to command all Confederate vessels defending Hampton Roads and its tributaries with the title of flag officer. The CSS *Virginia* would be his flagship.

"Buchanan was a typical product of the old-time quarter deck, as indomitably courageous as [British Admiral Lord] Nelson, and as arbitrary," recalled Lieutenant Eggleston. "I don't think the junior officer or sailor ever lived with nerve sufficient to disobey an order given by the old man in person."

Mallory instructed Buchanan: "The *Virginia* is a novelty in naval construction, is untried, and her powers unknown, and the Department will not give specific orders as to her attack upon the enemy."

The secretary did, however, encourage the flag officer to test that ancient and fearsome weapon of Mediterranean rowing galleys—the ram—which

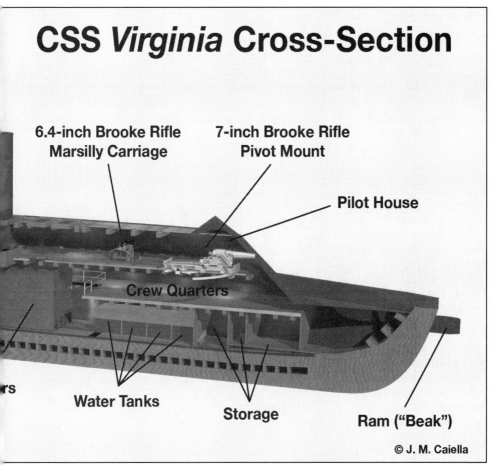

CSS *Virginia* Cross-Section

6.4-inch Brooke Rifle Marsilly Carriage

7-inch Brooke Rifle Pivot Mount

Pilot House

Crew Quarters

Water Tanks

Storage

Ram ("Beak")

© J. M. Caiella

now propelled by steam, had returned to action after three centuries. "Like the bayonet charge of infantry," ramming might compensate for scarcity of ammunition, and would be formidable even without guns.

The Confederacy had suffered painful reverses in February 1862. In the West, Gen. Ulysses S. Grant took Forts Henry and Donelson; Nashville was lost along with most of Tennessee and all of Kentucky. Grant closed in on Pittsburg Landing near Shiloh Church while Rebel armies regrouped at Corinth, Mississippi, to oppose him.

Union Brig. Gen. Ambrose Burnside captured Roanoke Island, North Carolina. The troops were transported and supported by elements of the North Atlantic Blockading Squadron under Flag Officer Louis M. Goldsborough. Federal control had been established over the strategically vital sounds and outer banks along with the southern end of the Dismal Swamp Canal.

The USS *Merrimack* was commissioned in February 1856, the lead ship of six *Merrimack*-class heavy frigates. She cruised the Caribbean, Western Europe, and coasts of Central and South America before returning to Norfolk in 1860 for overhaul. In April 1861, Navy Secretary Gideon Welles tried desperately to extract *Merrimack* before Virginia militia overran the navy yard. On 17 April, the day Virginia seceded, engineers managed to get the frigate's engines started, but a frightened and drunk yard commander refused to let her go. Three days later, Union personnel set yard and vessels alight and fled. (nhhc)

Burnside threatened to isolate Norfolk from Richmond, and both from railroads south; he endangered Maj. Gen. Benjamin Huger's army and Gosport Shipyard. Roanoke Island "ought to have been defended by all the means in the power of the Government," wrote Brig. Gen. Henry A. Wise. "It was the key to all the rear defenses of Norfolk."

With Union naval forces in Hampton Roads reduced by the North Carolina expedition, Mallory urged Buchanan to take advantage of means and opportunity for a decided blow. "Our utmost exertions" are demanded. "Action—prompt and successful action" must follow. "I congratulate you upon it, and know that your judgment and gallantry will meet all just expectations."

The navy secretary had grand visions for this revolutionary new weapon. "Could you pass Old Point [Comfort] and make a dashing cruise on the Potomac as far as Washington, its effect upon the public mind would be important to the cause," he suggested to Buchanan. A subsequent letter of March 7 asked: "Can the *Virginia* steam to New York and attack and burn the city?"

Presuming good weather and smooth seas, Mallory did not doubt *Virginia* could destroy the Brooklyn Navy Yard with its magazines, all the lower city, and much shipping. Bankers would withdraw their capital from the city. The enemy could never recover. Peace would inevitably follow. "Such an event would eclipse all the glories of the combats of the sea. . . . [and] would do more to achieve our immediate independence than would the results of many campaigns. Can the ship go there? Please give me your views."

Buchanan knew better, but he did have a plan. In late February, the flag officer met with Maj. Gen. John B. Magruder, commander of the Army of the Peninsula, to arrange joint operations against Union Camp Butler and Newport News Point. Anchored there and blocking the James River leading to Richmond were the sailing warships USS *Cumberland* and USS *Congress* along with one small gunboat and formidable land batteries within point blank range.

Buchanan intended to sally forth in *Virginia* accompanied by gunboats *Beaufort* and *Raleigh*. "My plan is to destroy the Frigates first, if possible," he wrote Magruder, "and then turn my attention to the battery on shore. I sincerely hope that acting together we may be successful in destroying many of the enemy."

Typical of meager pickings the Confederacy scraped together for its fledgling navy, *Beaufort* and *Raleigh* were small, iron-hulled, propeller steamers built for canals and inland waterways. Both mounted a single rifled 32-pounder in the bow, with magazines and boilers above the waterline exposed to shot.

Lieutenant William H. Parker commanded *Beaufort* with 35 officers and men; Lt. Joseph W. Alexander captained *Raleigh*. They had just participated in the "mosquito fleet" futilely defending Roanoke Island from Goldsborough's warships before fleeing up the Dismal Swamp Canal to become tenders for *Virginia*.

Buchanan's command included three other hastily converted gunboats bottled up in the James River above Newport News. *Patrick Henry* and *Jamestown* were sister ships—paddle-wheel coastal steamers with walking-beam engines. They were two of the larger and better constructed vessels seized by Confederates, almost as large as *Virginia*.

"*Patrick Henry*," recalled an officer, "was not at all fitted for a man-of-war, but we had to take what we could get, and by taking off her upper cabins, strengthening her decks, etc., made her answer pretty well." One-inch iron sheathing provided superficial protection to boilers and engines. She carried bow and stern pivot guns, and five guns in each broadside, 32- and 64-pounders.

Jamestown, similarly constructed but more lightly armed, carried two 32-pounder rifles. The third vessel,

Franklin Buchanan, Capt. and Acting Flag Officer, CSN, (1800-1874) was a crusty old salt with 45 adventurous years at sea. His maternal grandfather Thomas McKean signed the Declaration of Independence. Buchanan was first Superintendent of the Naval School (later Academy) at Annapolis in 1845. Assuming his native state would leave the Union, Buchanan resigned his captain's commission in April 1861. When Maryland failed to secede, he requested reinstatement to the U. S. Navy, but the new navy secretary abhorred traitors and dismissed him. Buchanan became the Confederacy's only full admiral. He made his last, futile stand commanding the ironclad CSS *Tennessee* against Admiral David G. Farragut at the Battle of Mobile Bay, August 5, 1864. (nhhc)

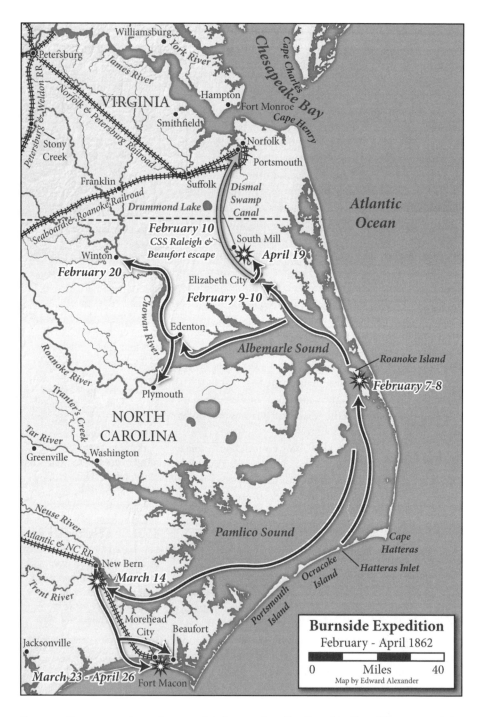

Burnside Expedition

February - April 1862

0   Miles   40

Map by Edward Alexander

Burnside Expedition— An underappreciated campaign, the Burnside Expedition secured the Carolina Sounds and Outer Banks for the Union, provided refuge for blockaders, interrupted Southern coastal commerce, occupied scarce Rebel troops and resources, and threatened Norfolk and Richmond from behind.

Teaser, was an aging steam tugboat mounting one bow gun. Commander John R. Tucker commanded the squadron and *Patrick Henry* with Lt. Joseph N. Barney in charge of *Jamestown* and Lt. William A. Webb in *Teaser*.

The plan called for General Magruder to assault Camp Butler from landward while Buchanan with *Virginia*, *Beaufort*, and *Raleigh* attacked up the Roads from the east, and Tucker's squadron descended the James from the northwest. Tucker was directed to come downriver before dawn on the morning of attack, ready to dash by Union batteries and join the fray. Yankees ashore and afloat would be trapped in a three-way pincer.

But on March 3, Magruder wrote to Buchanan: "It is too late to co-operate with my army in any manner with the Merrimac, even if the [muddy] roads will admit it, which they will not, for the enemy is very heavily re-enforced both at Newport News and Fort Monroe" with an estimated six regiments of infantry and six batteries of light artillery. He had intelligence that 30,000 men would land at Newport News before March 5.

Magruder also had been ordered to augment General Huger across the Roads in Norfolk with at least 5,000 men and two batteries. Reports indicated the enemy was preparing to swarm up the Dismal Swamp Canal and attack the city from the rear. Secretary of War Judah P. Benjamin wrote: "We do not believe that you [Magruder] are in the slightest danger of an attack at present, either in front or by being outflanked by naval forces," a conclusion with which Magruder disagreed.

Virginia could make no impression on Newport News anyway, thought Magruder. Only concentrated fire from many ships would persuade enemy troops to evacuate the batteries, while the mere presence of his meager army force "would incur a risk of disaster without any corresponding advantage."

Furthermore, *Virginia* could be injured by a chance shot at this critical time. But even if *Virginia* destroyed all vessels at Newport News Point, it would do little good. Better to station the ironclad above the point as a floating battery blocking Union gunboats from coming up the James and anchoring the Confederate army's right flank on the river.

Magruder concluded his letter to Buchanan with apparent frustration: "It would have been glorious" if *Virginia* had intercepted Yankee reinforcements as they were being landed from commercial transports. Now, he was compelled to withdraw his little army back to a shorter line on the Warwick River. "Any dependence

John Bankhead Magruder, Maj. Gen., CSA (1807-1871), commander of the Army of the Peninsula, famously defeated Union forces at Big Bethel in June 1861. He would soon confront McClellan's advance up the Peninsula, stalling him at Yorktown. But like Huger, Magruder would be criticized for leadership in the Seven Days Campaign. He finished the war administering the Trans-Mississippi Department. Magruder was known as "Prince John" for his elaborate uniforms. (loc)

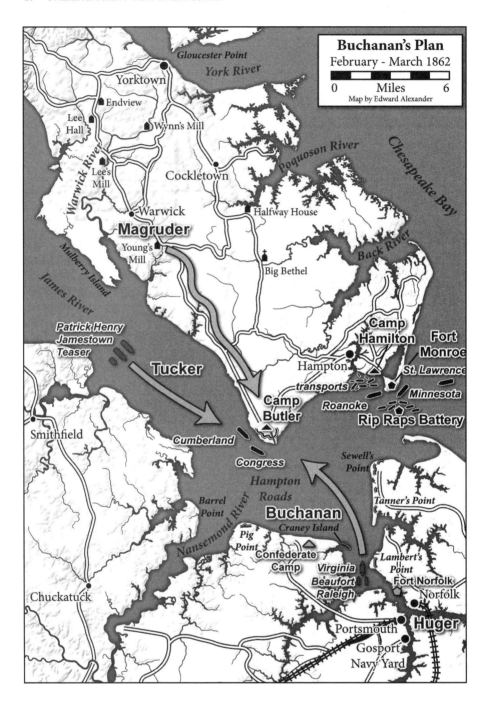

BUCHANAN'S PLAN— Flag Officer Buchannan planned a joint operation with General Magruder to sink Union warships off Newport News Point and capture Camp Butler with its garrison. Threatened by Union reinforcements, Magruder backed out. Buchannan would proceed without the army.

upon me, so far as Newport News is concerned, is at an end." Magruder's fears would be realized just a few weeks later as Maj. Gen. George McClellan's mighty host descended on the peninsula.

Flag Officer Buchanan was undaunted. He learned from a March 3 edition of the *New York Times* that the USS *Monitor* passed her sea trials. She could be expected in Hampton Roads any day. He would get *Virginia* underway as soon as possible and do as much damage as possible before additional enemy reinforcements—land or water—arrived.

Ideally, *Virginia* would destroy or chase the wooden U.S. Navy out of the Roads, defend Norfolk and Gosport, disrupt the blockade, prevent Army of the Potomac advances by water toward Richmond, and secure the south bank of the peninsula. Though not Washington or New York, these achievements would be major victories for one thrown-together warship, two converted merchant steamers, and a handful of puny gunboats.

Buchanan scheduled the attack for Thursday night, March 6, but civilian harbor pilots refused to guide this big, clumsy, deep-draft vessel in the dark through narrow river channels with difficult currents and from which marker lights and buoys had been removed. The storm caused additional delay since *Virginia* could operate only in calm waters. Meanwhile, Norfolk

The sailing frigate USS *Congress* and the sloop-of-war USS *Cumberland* were both commissioned in 1842 and little changed in concept from America's original frigates like the USS *Constitution* (1797), Old Ironsides. *Congress* cruised the Mediterranean, South Atlantic, and Pacific Oceans, and along the west coast during the Mexican War. (nhhc)

William Harwar Parker, Lt., CSN (1826-1896) had a 24-year, globe-straddling sea career starting at age 15. He participated in amphibious landings and naval shore battery operations at Veracruz during the Mexican War, meeting Ulysses Grant, Joseph Johnston, and Robert Lee. His postings ranged from the 74-gun ship-of-the-line USS *North Carolina* to his command at Hampton Roads of the 85-foot gunboat, CSS *Beaufort*. Parker would become the commandant of the Confederate Naval Academy and author of the classic memoir *Recollections of a Naval Officer*. (nhhc)

papers published articles of disinformation to the effect that the ironclad was a failure and would not be able to accomplish anything.

Unknown to Confederates, the USS *Monitor* was approaching Cape Henry when, about 11:00 a.m., Buchanan hoisted his flag officer's red pennant on *Virginia* and commanded his warships to get underway. All workmen, some making final adjustments to armor and machinery, were ordered off.

Virginia, *Beaufort*, and *Raleigh* cast off as mechanics jumped ashore. The little squadron pulled away, stood downriver, and cleared for action. Only a few of Buchanan's senior lieutenants knew of his plans while most of the crew thought this was just a shakedown cruise.

Years later, Army Captain Norris recalled witnessing this "huge, unwieldly make-shift" craft steaming out on a beautiful morning "officered with the very cream of the old navy, and manned by as gallant a crew as ever fought in a good cause—Southern born almost to a man. . . ."

She was, continued Norris, "freighted down to the very guards with the tearful prayers and hopes of a whole people," fighting heroically against overwhelming odds that they might govern their own soil in their own way. "Every man and officer well understood the desperate hazards of the approaching fight; the utter feebleness of their ship, and the terrible efficiency of the enemy's magnificent fleet. . . ."

"The weather was fair, the wind light, and the tide half flood," wrote Lieutenant Parker in *Beaufort*. Nearly every man, woman and child in Norfolk and Portsmouth gathered at Sewell's Point, Craney Island, and other vantage points to observe the great naval combat.

All shore batteries were manned. All work in public and private shipyards was suspended while those remaining behind thronged churches and offered prayers. Everything that would float from army tugboat to oysterman's skiff was loaded to the water's edge with spectators.

"A great stillness came over the land," continued Parker. Caps and handkerchiefs waved from river banks, "but no voice broke the silence of the scene; all hearts were too full for utterance; an attempt at cheering would have ended in tears, for all realized the fact that here was to be tried the great experiment of the ram and iron-clad in naval warfare."

Many thought *Virginia* would sink with all hands enclosed in an "iron-plated coffin" as soon as she rammed a vessel. Nevertheless, concluded Parker, those about to do battle went coolly about their duties.

Buchanan intended to be in the Roads by 1:30 p.m. at full tide for optimum maneuverability in deeper channels. Final orders to his captains included a new signal consisting of the flag for the number one hoisted above the commodore's pennant, meaning "sink before you surrender."

The CSS *Virginia* and the USS *Monitor* converged on Hampton Roads cleared for action. Their journeys to this point had been as unprecedented as the impending battle.

Joseph Nicholson Barney, Lt., CSN (1818-1899) was the grandson of navy Commodore Joshua Barney, renowned veteran of the Revolution and War of 1812. Joseph joined the navy in 1835 rising to lieutenant by 1861. Following the Battles of Hampton Roads, Barney scuttled *Jamestown* to block the James River. He removed her guns and crewmen to Drewry's Bluff where they played a major role in turning back Union warships, including the USS *Monitor*, on May 15, 1862. (nhhc)

It Strikes Me There's Something in It

CHAPTER THREE

LATE SUMMER, 1861

On a steamy day in August 1861, the new Secretary of the United States Navy, Gideon Welles, met with fellow Connecticuter and friend, Cornelius S. Bushnell, at the Willard Hotel across from the White House. Welles handed over a copy of legislation he was proposing. Congress sat in special session to approve President Lincoln's executive actions raising troops and committing funds to suppress the rebellion, and Welles was anxious that his bill also be considered. Bushnell, an influential railroad executive and shipbuilder from New Haven, agreed to lobby the matter on the hill.

"Much attention has been given within the last few years to the subject of floating batteries, or iron-clad steamers," Welles reported to Congress. "The ingenuity and inventive faculties of our own countrymen have also been stimulated by recent occurrences." It was, however, a subject full of difficulty and doubt. Large-scale experiments in England and France had experienced limited success. "Yet it was evident that a new and material element in maritime warfare was developing itself, and demanded immediate attention."

The secretary was overseeing an urgent, immense, unprecedented warship procurement and building program while instigating a nearly impossible, continent-wide blockade. It would not be advisable in the current crisis to commit heavy expenditures for experiments on unproven technology. He therefore recommended appointment of a "proper and competent board" to inquire into and report on the subject before Congress considered larger appropriations for operational vessels.

John Ericsson holds a *Monitor* model in this monument dedicated on the centennial of his birth, 1906, in Battery Park, New York City. The pedestal inscription reads: "The City Of New York / Erects This Statue To The / Memory Of A Citizen Whose / Genius Has Contributed / To The Greatness Of The / Republic And The Progress / Of The World." (wmpd)

Gideon Welles (1802-1878), Secretary of the U. S. Navy, was a prominent Connecticut journalist and politician with strong anti-slavery views. A former Democrat, he joined the new Republican Party and supported Abraham Lincoln in the 1860 election. Welles was a natural choice when the president needed a New England representative in the cabinet. Beginning in 1861 with 76 ships and 7,600 sailors, the secretary expanded the navy tenfold. (nhhc)

Like other department heads, Gideon Welles—a lawyer, newspaperman, and party loyalist—was appointed by the president primarily for political and regional balance in the cabinet. His only navy experience had been as civilian head of the Bureau of Provisions and Clothing in the 1840s, which at least provided familiarity with terminology and procedures.

Welles was known to be excitable and voluble; he was accused by some of lacking tact or sympathy, with an arbitrary, inflexible mind. His old brown wig, which no longer matched the snowy beard, meandered around his dome as if it had a mind of its own. The urbane Secretary of State, William Seward, among others, considered Welles unsophisticated and comical, and frequently opposed him in the president's councils.

Nevertheless, Welles proved to be an astute, experienced politician as well as a meticulous and indefatigable administrator who prized order and procedure. Admiral David D. Porter credited Welles with superior judgment along with "coolness and placidity of temper." Lincoln most of all came to rely on "Father Neptune" for steadfast loyalty, honesty, and passion. Leading a naval revolution, Welles would contribute greatly to victory.

A "distinguished citizen of Massachusetts" entered a letter into the congressional record supporting the Welles legislation. Mr. E. H. Derby urged the necessity for acquiring "mail-clad steamers—a subject which he has thoroughly examined." Neglect of this opportunity "will expose us to serious losses, obloquy, and disgrace." The British had tested and confirmed that 4.5-inch iron plates were impervious to shot and shell even from the best Armstrong and Whitworth 100-pounder cannon. They had ceased building wooden warships altogether.

"England and France will, by the close of this year, have twenty to thirty iron-clad steam ships, each of which could pass into Boston or New York with impunity, and possibly destroy either city. Unless we have means to meet them, France and England may be able to dictate terms as to the southern blockade. With such steamers we can, with little or no loss, recover Charleston, Savannah, Pensacola, Galveston, Mobile, and New Orleans. . . . [I] trust you will grasp a weapon so essential to our country at this moment."

Iowa Senator James Grimes introduced the bill: "We need a more effective blockade. . . . Scoundrels North, as well as scoundrels South, are carrying on an unlawful trade in fraud of our revenue." Pirates and sea rovers must be captured; Southern harbors and forts must be retaken; commerce must be protected, and Northern harbors defended.

"Suppose England, in her love for cotton, should forget the duties which she owes to mankind and attempt to break our blockade, and we should get into trouble with her: what is to become of our northern cities and our cities upon the coast?" Grimes wished to protect his country and "preserve it in all its parts."

European navies had grappled for decades with simultaneous revolutions in warship construction, propulsion, and armament. Military tradeoffs included size, speed, survivability, cruising range, strategy, and tactics. Then there were political concerns of finance, industrial infrastructure, patronage, and public opinion. Outcomes that seem obvious in hindsight appeared murky at the time.

In 1855, Secretary of War Jefferson Davis had dispatched a commission including Capt. George McClellan to observe the Crimean War. They witnessed the siege of Sevastopol and reported in engineering detail as British and French ironclad floating batteries, mortar vessels, and gunboats reduced Russian forts at Kinburn to rubble while easily deflecting savage return fire from heavy shore guns.

The report's conclusion: "Steam-propelling power, the rifle cannon, long range and heavy caliber, in wrought-iron vessels, are the new features. . . . It is the bounden duty of the officers of our army and navy to study this branch of the art of war. . . ." Wooden warships dependent on wind, armed with lighter smoothbores, had never been effective against stout walls. But now, the United States must improve shore fortifications and must devise "floating armament" to drive future ironclad invaders from national waters.

Europeans struggled to produce armored vessels that could sail, steam, and fight in heavy seas. France led the way in 1859 with the impressive ironclad frigate *La Gloire*, followed in 1860 by the magnificent British HMS *Warrior*, an all-iron vessel representing the epitome of contemporary naval engineering.

But these prototypes had serious shortcomings: high cost, limited cruising range, frequent industrial maintenance. Wooden hulls of equal displacement were lighter, generally faster, more flexible and survivable in heavy seas, and not as susceptible to rust and fouling.

Cornelius Scranton Bushnell (1829-1896) rebuilt the bankrupt New Haven and New London Railroad, and by 1861, was president of the line. He teamed with noted naval architect Samuel Pook to develop the plans that became the ironclad USS *Galena*. (Pook also designed the famous Mississippi River ironclads called "Pook Turtles.") Post-war, Bushnell was an organizer of the Union Pacific Railroad. (nhhc)

Contemporary iron was subject to inconsistencies in manufacturing processes and ingredients. Bad iron could be as brittle, splintering, and fatal under fire as wood, perhaps more so.

The U.S. Navy was in the forefront of developments in steam propulsion and naval armaments. The 1840s and 1850s saw a vigorous program of modernization and new construction, much of it supported by Senator Stephen R. Mallory, chairman of the Committee on Naval Affairs and future Confederate Secretary of the Navy.

Among other programs, Mallory sponsored a bill for construction of six large, swift, and powerful new screw frigates. The lead ship became the USS *Merrimack*, the pride of the U.S. Navy, followed by sister ships *Wabash*, *Roanoke*, *Niagara*, *Minnesota* and *Colorado*, all named for rivers.

The *Merrimack* frigates were considered even by European competitors among the best of their type; they would form the wooden backbone of the wartime U.S. Navy. These traditional but transitional models were designed for speed under sail with auxiliary steam for calms, contrary winds, and close maneuvering.

Steam engines were not sufficiently reliable, efficient, or robust to be the primary, much less the only, propulsive power at sea. They were rapidly improving, but after millennia of development, sail technology reached its apogee at mid-century and still ruled the waves.

The rising generation of technically savvy American officers had been content to allow others to pursue costly experiments in armor protection. In America, wood was inexpensive and plentiful; iron was expensive and difficult to produce, the reverse of Great Britain. Public and congressional disinterest generated limited funding.

The United States had little incentive to build a large seagoing force—no far-flung empire to defend, no neighboring menace, and until recently, no imminent danger from across the Atlantic. Naval strategy focused on harbor and coastal defense with a requisite number of fast cruisers to protect commerce in distant waters.

John Augustus Griswold (1818–1872) matured with the fledgling iron industry in Troy, New York, where he founded one of the largest and most successful iron and steel works in the nation. Griswold helped finance *Monitor's* construction along with later *Monitor*-class ironclads. He contributed to three New York infantry regiments and founded the 21st New York "Griswold Light Cavalry." Griswold served in the U. S. House of Representatives from 1863 to 1869. (nhhc)

The first ocean-going ironclad, the French *Gloire* or "Glory" (257' long, 56' beam, 28' draft) was launched in 1859 in response to advances in naval artillery that rendered wood hulls increasingly obsolete. French General Henri-Joseph Paixhans developed explosive shells in the 1820s while refinements in metallurgy and manufacture produced larger guns, and improved bore rifling increased accuracy and range. (loc)

HMS *Warrior* (420' long, 58' beam, 27' draft) was the first armor-plated, all iron-hulled warship, built in response to France's *Gloire*. She also was of standard frigate, broadside design, but huge and fast for her time with powerful guns. *Warrior* became obsolete following the 1871 launch of the mastless and more capable HMS *Devastation*. She is now a fully restored museum ship in Portsmouth, England. (nhhc)

Secession altered the strategic seascape dramatically as crisis rippled across the Atlantic. Britons experienced cotton shortages, economic and commercial disruptions, and massive unemployment leading to domestic unrest and political turmoil. Echoing the Revolution and War of 1812, conflicts in international law flared involving the boundaries of neutrality, the blockade, trade in arms, munitions and warships, privateering and commerce raiding. Old enmities resurfaced on both sides while British leaders considered intervention, with force if necessary.

The specter of a third war between the United States and the world's most powerful nation—armed with big, seagoing ironclads—became real and immediate. The *Philadelphia Examiner* reflected an aroused Northern public opinion when the editors thought it curious that the United States should be behind the age. "If we intend to have a national naval force worthy of our power and pretensions, we shall have to . . . build iron-cased vessels, as France and England have done, and are doing."

However, the most immediate threats were Confederate ironclads under construction in Norfolk, New Orleans, and Nashville, particularly the former *Merrimack*. Despite enemy efforts at secrecy, sympathizers, exchanged prisoners, slaves, and freedmen fleeing daily across Hampton Roads kept Secretary Welles well informed. He also read Southern newspapers.

The *Mobile Register* boasted that the new Confederate weapon "would be a floating fortress that will be able to defeat the whole Navy of the United States and bombard its cities." With her great size, strength, powerful engines, and invulnerable iron casing, she would easily destroy or disperse the blockading fleet. "She could entertain herself by throwing bombs into fortress Monroe, even without risk. We hope soon to hear that she is ready to commence her avenging career on the seas."

Congress passed and President Lincoln signed the Welles legislation on August 3, 1861. As recommended, it directed the secretary to appoint a board of three skillful naval officers to investigate plans and specifications for

Captain Joseph Smith, USN (1790-1877) joined at age 19 and served almost 60 years. He was severely wounded at the Battle of Lake Champlain (1814). Captain Smith commanded the 74-gun ship-of-the-line USS *Ohio* and later the Mediterranean Squadron with the position title of Commodore and the USS *Cumberland* as flagship. From 1846 until 1869, he served as Chief of the Bureau of Yards and Docks. Smith was promoted to rear admiral when those ranks were established in 1862. (nhhc)

Captain Hiram Paulding, USN (1797-1878) sailed the globe in an adventurous half-century career, retiring in 1857. Like Captain Smith, Paulding commanded a squadron and would be addressed as commodore. President Lincoln called him back in 1861 to assist in the naval buildup, taking charge of the New York Navy Yard. He also would be promoted to rear admiral. (nhhc)

constructing "iron or steel-clad steamships or steam batteries" and upon their recommendation, to cause one or more prototypes to be built. The act appropriated $1.5 million for that purpose.

The secretary's technical advisors, including Chief Naval Constructor John Lenthall, were both skeptical and too busy to conduct time-consuming experiments in what presumably would be a short war. So, Welles selected senior line officers to the "Ironclad Board." Commodores Joseph Smith, age 71, and Hiram Paulding, age 63, were distinguished combat veterans of the War of 1812, crusty old salts of the wood and canvas navy. Commander Charles H. Davis, age 54, was the third member.

The Navy Department advertised for proposals for vessels either of iron or wood and iron for sea or river service, between 10- and 16-feet draft, to carry armament of 80 to 120 tons, with provisions and stores for 165 to 300 persons for 60 days and coal for 8 days. By early September, 16 offers ranging from conservative to crazy (including a "rubber-clad") had been received.

"We approach the subject with diffidence," stated the board, "having no experience and but scanty knowledge in this branch of naval architecture. . . . it is very likely that some of our conclusions may prove erroneous." Like most senior warriors, these men were conservative but not, as often accused, opposed to progress. They fully supported the advantages of steam and propeller propulsion as the industry developed.

But amidst technological uncertainty and inexperience, they demanded reasonable assurances that new ideas perform well against the nation's enemies while conserving the lives of her sons. Unlike engineers and scientists, their concerns were intensely practical and experiential, not theoretical.

"Opinions differ amongst naval and scientific men as to the policy of adopting the iron armature for ships-of-war," concluded the board's report. "But whilst other nations are endeavoring to perfect them, we must not remain idle."

Although current technology offered uncertain advantages for long-range, sea-going cruisers, smaller vessels could be formidable adjuncts to land fortifications in harbor and river defense. "We consider iron-clad vessels of light draught, or floating batteries thus shielded, as very important; and we feel. . .the necessity of them on some of our rivers and inlets to enforce obedience to the laws."

Some suggested that the navy should contract with British firms to have ironclads built. They had better facilities and greater experience, including the ability to roll iron plate up to 4 inches thick. They were ready and willing; the expense probably would be less than at home.

But the board said no. "A difficulty might arise with the British government. . . ." Reliance on a foreign supplier, particularly this powerful former foe and current rival, might be construed as weakness; it could be an argument in favor of their intervention to the advantage of the Confederacy. "We are of opinion that every people or nation who can maintain a navy should be capable of constructing it themselves."

Given the urgency, the board took the radical step of recommending three designs to be produced simultaneously on a spectrum of increasing risk. The most conservative and most practicable featured a fully seaworthy, wooden-hulled sailing vessel with iron plating, auxiliary steam engine, and broadside battery. Conceptually like *Gloire* and *Warrior*, the future USS *New Ironsides* traded higher cost and longer construction time for lower technological uncertainty while countering the foreign ironclad threat.

The second design—submitted by Secretary Welles's friend, Cornelius Bushnell—also was a conventional sail/steam frigate but was smaller, with a shallower draft, and armored with interlocking strips of wrought iron in a manner not yet tried. She would become the USS *Galena*. The final board selection was a leap in the dark.

The board's acceptance of Bushnell's design carried a caveat: He was required to resolve concerns about buoyancy and stability in his innovative design given the weight of armor. Bushnell took the advice of a friend and traveled to New York to consult Swedish engineer John Ericsson.

The intense, stocky Ericsson had a long career in Sweden, England, and America designing, building, and improving steam engines—mining and drainage machines, refrigerators for breweries and distilleries, steam-powered fire engines, locomotives, and marine engines. He produced a host of inventions, including the shipboard steam condenser, and collected numerous patents.

Mechanical engineering was an emerging discipline without strict professional standards or formal accreditation as now understood. Enthusiastic amateurs, civilian and military, experimented on existing mechanisms, pushing the boundaries in incremental

Charles Henry Davis, Commander, USN (1807-1877) was seconded to the Coast Survey (now National Geodetic Survey) in 1846. Researching tides and currents, he located a wreck-strewn uncharted shoal off the New York coast. In November 1861, Davis would be promoted to captain and acting flag officer in charge of the Western Gunboat Flotilla. In the summer of 1862, his squadron virtually eliminated Confederate naval presence on the Mississippi River at the Battle of Memphis, and then cooperated with Flag Officer David G. Farragut in an unsuccessful attack on Vicksburg. (nhhc)

improvements, often without fully comprehending the underlying science. Their results would be verified or rejected in an unhurried, sequential build-test-build process. More radical notions raised the odds of technical and financial failure.

With extensive experience but no formal education, Ericsson's talent tended toward drawing, planning, and calculating more than detailed tinkering and constructing. He gained respect among engineers, but also overreached and suffered notable setbacks. Success, the Swede painfully learned, depended as much on nontechnical factors such as political influence, economic resources, and public perception as on expertise; it required pull, persuasion, and performance.

In the renowned Liverpool and Manchester Railway locomotive trials of 1829, Ericsson's *Novelty* was the fastest entry but suffered boiler failures, losing to the iconic Stephenson's *Rocket* that sparked the railroad revolution. In 1837, Ericsson demonstrated his prototype screw propeller on the Thames, but the British Admiralty, not yet convinced of its practicality, took no action.

USS *New Ironsides* spent most of her career blockading Charleston and Wilmington, bombarding fortifications during several major naval attacks on the harbors. Although heavy shore batteries struck many times, they never significantly damaged the ship or injured the crew. Her sailors participated in the naval battalion that attacked the northeast bastion during the Second Battle of Fort Fisher in January 1865; eight were awarded the Medal of Honor. (nhhc)

Nevertheless, the propeller would begin to replace side paddle wheels for driving steam warships. It was far less vulnerable to enemy fire, allowed steam machinery to be located safely below the waterline, and opened the ship's sides for guns. Ericsson failed to file first for the English patent, losing it to another inventor.

In 1839, U.S. Navy Captain and naval innovator Robert F. Stockton lured Ericsson to the United States and then convinced Congress to authorize the nation's first screw-propelled steam warship with the Swede as designer and construction supervisor. The resulting USS *Princeton* had enormous success until one of the big guns exploded during a demonstration cruise on the Potomac in February 1844, killing six including the Secretaries of State and Navy, and nearly killing President John Tyler.

Stockton himself had altered Ericsson's design for the cannon, weakening its structure, but he sidestepped blame while undeservedly implicating the supervising engineer and failing to pay for his services. Public backlash

USS *Galena* reported to Hampton Roads in April 1862 to support the Peninsula Campaign. Note that original masts and sails have been removed except for a lookout station forward while a conning tower has been added aft. Widely considered a failure, *Galena* would be reconstructed in 1863 without most of her armor and in 1864 transferred west where she participated in the Battle of Mobile Bay. *Galena* was scrapped in 1872. (nhhc)

blackened the reputations of both ship and engineer. An embittered Ericsson continued experimenting and building but shunned the navy until Cornelius Bushnell knocked on his door. Bushnell would conclude that Ericsson was "a full electric battery himself" becoming one of the inventor's staunchest proponents.

Detractors like Capt. John Rogers also would emerge: "Mr. Ericsson is in some respects a peculiar man. . . . He has abundance of genius and resources—but he is not always sound in his conclusions—at the same time he is so confident and abundantly fortified in arguments that the danger of falling into his way of thinking is very great. . . . Mr. Ericsson is the man who must be kept from doing harm, by insisting upon experimental proof of what he advances or proposes."

Ericsson reviewed Bushnell's ironclad plans and pronounced the design theoretically sound. Then, the Swede surprised the visitor with his own plans for, as Bushnell later wrote, "a floating battery absolutely impregnable to the heaviest shot or shell." These included a pasteboard model of a small iron raft with—its most radical innovation—a revolving turret enclosing a tiny cannon.

Ericsson explained how quickly and powerfully she could be built. The almost-submerged design—inspired by Swedish lumber rafts—had been percolating in his mind for years. He proudly exhibited a medal and letter of thanks from Emperor Napoleon III, who had considered the idea in 1854 but did not pursue it.

Ericsson never claimed to have invented the turret, only to have improved the concept and first deployed it. The idea of a revolving gun platform, open or closed, had been debated for nearly a century; it was, he said, "a device familiar to all well-informed naval artillerists." An American inventor in 1843 proposed a metallic revolving

On May 15, 1862, the USS *Galena* led a squadron including the USS *Monitor* and three gunboats up the James River only to be stopped by Confederate batteries on Drewry's Bluff seven miles below the capital. This photo of her port side shortly after the battle shows two IX-inch Dahlgren smoothbores and the unique horizontally-laid interlocking iron side armor, armored gun port shutters, and boat davits. At least one enemy shot hole is stoppered with a wooden plug near the waterline, bottom left center. (nhhc)

This 1862 engraving for *Harper's Weekly* depicts the USS *Galena's* gundeck. Like most wartime drawings of its kind, the one is out of scale, leaving the impression of a much less cluttered, crowded, and constricted space than it was. During the Battle of Drewry's Bluff, furious plunging fire penetrated the light deck armor overhead, killing 14 and wounding 10; she took 45 hits before withdrawing. (nhhc)

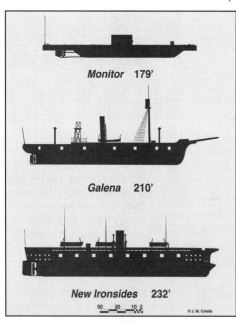

A scale comparison of the first three Union ironclads. *Graphic by J. M. Caiella.* (jmc)

fort for land or water and held a relevant patent for which Ericsson would voluntarily pay royalties. A British rival had produced a superior design, which would supersede Ericsson's in future developments.

Bushnell was delighted with the model and took it with Ericsson's permission to Hartford where Welles vacationed. He astounded the secretary by saying that now the country was safe: "I had found a battery which would make us master of the situation so far as the ocean was concerned." The idea possessed, recalled Welles, "extraordinary and valuable features" applicable to coast and river blockade; it involved "a revolution in naval warfare." Welles dispatched Bushnell with the model to Washington.

As partners, Bushnell enlisted two other wealthy and influential industrialists: John Griswold and Congressman John Winslow, both Albany, New York, iron manufacturers. They brought crucial financial backing, business connections, and friends in the capital including Secretary of State Seward. Carrying a letter of introduction from Seward, the three partners went straight to the president at the White House.

Lincoln, ever fascinated by gadgets, "was at once greatly pleased with the simplicity of the plan," wrote Bushnell, and agreed to accompany them to a meeting of the Ironclad Board the next morning, September 13. "All [board members] were surprised at the novelty of the plan. Some advised trying it; others ridiculed it." The president remarked: "All I have to say is what the girl said when she put her foot into the stocking, 'It strikes me there's something in it.'"

Despite this endorsement, continued Bushnell, the board was not receptive. "The air had been thick with croakings that the department was about to father another Ericsson failure," referring to the *Princeton* incident. Commander Davis, the most scientifically literate of the group, told Bushnell to "take the little thing home and worship it, as it would not be idolatry because it was made in the image of nothing in the heaven above or the earth below or the waters under the earth."

But Bushnell was determined to vindicate his new friend and move the project forward. Returning to Ericsson in New York, he whitewashed the board's reaction, claiming they just required a few technical clarifications, and convinced the prickly inventor to come to Washington. Face to face with the board, Ericsson was not welcomed. A skeptical Commodore Smith is said to have exclaimed that the proposed vessel "would upset and place her crew in the inconvenient and undesirable position of submarine divers."

With Welles's encouragement, the board finally succumbed to persuasion. Ericsson's plan addressed the critical requirement: a combat-ready craft suitable for restricted waters to be rapidly constructed and deployed. In its favor were presumed invulnerability, small size, shallow draft, and limited exposed target area.

Worrisome unknowns included: over reliance on steam power, semi-submerged hull, questionable stability, and untried turret-mounted armament. Other compromises involved habitability, seaworthiness, and restricted space to operate and maintain guns and machinery. It was still an "experiment."

Ericsson claimed to have simply presented a theoretical demonstration concerning stability to "well-informed and experienced naval experts," convincing them that his design was practical and sound. One version has him concluding: "Gentlemen, after what I have said, I consider it to be your duty to the country to give me an order to build the vessel before I leave the room." Later that day, Secretary Welles promised him a contract.

John Ericsson died on March 8, 1889, the anniversary of the Battle of Hampton Roads. Responding to his wish to be buried in Sweden, the navy transported his remains on the cruiser USS *Baltimore* escorted by a squadron of warships. A hundred thousand people turned out for the funeral procession and departure ceremonies, including several *Monitor* veterans, as the fleet departed with a twenty-one-gun salute. (nhhc)

Not the Slightest Intention of Sinking

CHAPTER FOUR
OCTOBER 4, 1861 – MARCH 4, 1862

The contract signed on October 4, 1861, ordered an "Iron Clad Shot-Proof Steam Battery" of the finest materials and workmanship. John Ericsson and his backers were to deliver the vessel complete and ready for service (excepting guns, ammunition, coal, and stores) within the proposed—and unprecedented—span of 100 days for a price of $275,000. The terms also required masts, spars, sails and rigging—a stipulation that would be conveniently ignored.

Commodore Joseph Smith of the Ironclad Board also headed the Bureau of Yards and Docks and served as Ericsson's immediate supervisor. They exchanged numerous letters during construction in which the skeptical commodore prodded the engineer, made design suggestions, and asked pointed questions. "Excuse me for being so troublesome," he wrote early on, "but my great anxiety must plead my excuse."

The government would advance incremental payments during construction with 25% withheld pending successful trials. "In case of failure in any of the properties and points of the vessel as proposed," the product would be rejected, and previous payments refunded to the government. This type of performance guarantee had become standard in the relatively new practice of subcontracting civilian industrial firms to produce steam machinery for which navy shipyards had no capability.

The Ironclad Board took the—also unprecedented—step of requiring proof of performance not just in controlled trials but in the chaos of combat. The vessel would remain the investors' property and financial liability

Monitor's four-blade, cast-iron, nine-foot diameter propeller is on display in the Large Artifact Gallery of the *Monitor* Center. (mmp)

Robinson Woolen Hands, Third Assistant Engineer USN (1835-1865), was lost when *Monitor* sank on December 31, 1862. (nhhc)

going into its first battle with acceptance contingent on a successful outcome. John Winslow, the partner with the bulk of the money, hesitated on this point.

The irrepressible Swede, however, displayed utmost confidence, informing Smith that the decision to test under enemy fire was perfectly reasonable and proper: "If the structure cannot stand this test, then it is, indeed, worthless." Ericsson calculated that such a demonstration would be persuasive to both the public and politicians regarding future contracts (and so it would prove in the "*Monitor* mania" that followed). In any case, all concerned anticipated an immediate opportunity to fulfill this requirement with no extensive workups.

Ericsson lit the fuse on a frenetic and incredibly complex manufacturing process even before the contract was signed. With the partners' help, he orchestrated a conglomerate of nine contractors and multiple subcontractors working simultaneously in at least seven northeast cities to produce raw materials—angle iron, bar iron, plate iron, rivets—and finished components for assembly at Continental Ironworks in Greenpoint, New York, near Brooklyn.

Most of these firms clustered around New York City and Albany, centers of steam engine manufacturing, and Philadelphia, Trenton, and Baltimore for iron production. They applied facilities, methods, and materials in common use for locomotives and similar terrestrial products.

These Yankees possessed the breadth and depth of industrial capacity to produce an experimental iron vessel from scratch in a bit over 100 days. (It took Confederates nearly nine months to convert *Merrimack*.) The conglomeration constructed monitors of all types for the rest of the war.

Upon Ericsson's request, the navy assigned Chief Engineer Alban Crocker Stimers to superintend construction. Stimers represented that revolutionary and starkly dissimilar class of naval officer—steam engineers. Congress created the navy's Engineering Corps in 1842 with the commissioned officer ranks of engineer-in-chief, chief engineer, and assistant engineer.

In the millennia-old technology of sail and wood, seamen were generalists, their skills more instinct and experience than science or engineering. They focused always upward and outward while maneuvering the world's largest moving objects in masterful choreographies of sea, sky, and wind. But now down below in former cargo spaces, denizens of engine and boiler spaces

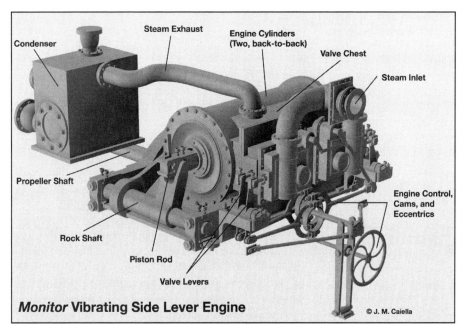

Condenser

Steam Exhaust

Engine Cylinders
(Two, back-to-back)

Valve Chest

Steam Inlet

Propeller Shaft

Engine Control,
Cams, and
Eccentrics

Rock Shaft

Piston Rod

Valve Levers

Monitor Vibrating Side Lever Engine

© J. M. Caiella

epitomized humanity's increasing mastery over nature. They looked entirely inward, mastering dirty, noisy, and dangerous machines, channeling manmade power into purposeful motion, which in reasonable conditions, took no heed of natural forces.

Specialists of the machine age, navy steam engineers had perhaps more in common with railroad counterparts than with line officers. Most trained through long apprenticeships in manufacturing and railroad machine shops, on merchant or navy steam vessels, before being certified by examination. They designed, acquired, installed, operated, and maintained steam machinery ashore and afloat. This mission, however vital, did not capture the ancient prestige of sailing and fighting the ship from the high rigging and exposed deck. Line officers still tended to think of engineers as mechanics.

Alban Stimers was well qualified, having advanced rapidly through varied assignments. He had been chief engineer of the USS *Merrimack* when she steamed into Norfolk in February 1860 to be decommissioned for a major overhaul of her troublesome engines. By some accounts, the engineer was as overconfident and overbearing as the inventor, but they worked well together. Stimers would not be an official member of *Monitor's* crew. However, at Ericsson's request, he accompanied them as an observer, playing a major role in the action.

Monitor's engine had two cylinders sharing a common barrel. The manifold at right admitted steam from the boilers. At lower right is the reversing gear control. *Graphic by J. M. Caiella.* (jmc)

USS *Monitor* Boilers.
Graphic by J. M. Caiella. (jmc)

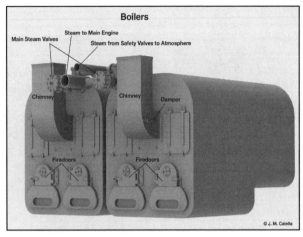

Monitor's keel was laid on October 25, 1861. Time and practicality compelled Ericsson to abandon some of his original concepts including the "steam gun" and "hydrostatic javelin" (a proto-torpedo), replaced by the readily available Dahlgren guns. The vessel's main deck became flat instead of sloping; the turret was cylindrical rather than hemispheric, both much easier to construct. He compromised on 1-inch plate iron for the turret because no domestic mill was prepared to produce 4-inch plate.

Sailors could lower and raise the anchor from within the hull without exposure to enemy fire. *Graphic by J. M. Caiella.* (jmc)

In the 1840s, Ericsson had crafted a compact, vibrating side-lever steam engine—with the cylinder horizontal rather than vertical—to accommodate cramped

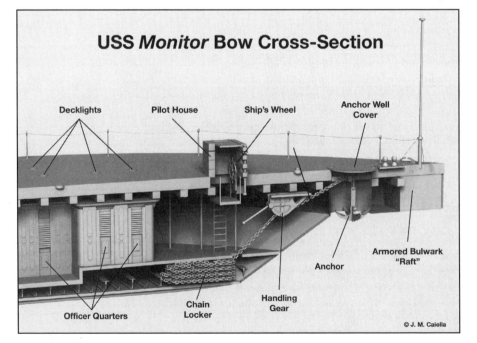

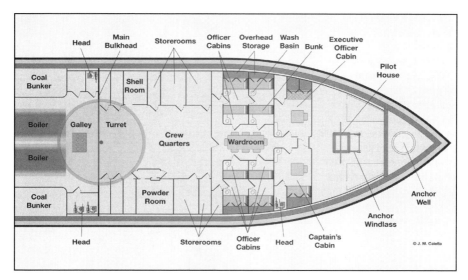

The layout of *Monitor's* living quarters and storage spaces. *Graphic by J. M. Caiella.* (jmc)

engineering spaces and bring vulnerable machinery below the waterline. *Monitor's* 30-ton engine had a single cylinder, 40 inches in diameter, driving two pistons.

The engine delivered 400 horsepower at full steam to the 9-foot propeller, driving the vessel at 9 knots. Two 14- by 9-foot boilers behind the galley stove were fueled by anthracite coal in bunkers to port and starboard, 40 tons each side, for 12 hours of steaming at full speed.

Built at Delamater Ironworks in New York City, the engine was ferried across the East River to Greenpoint and installed in the rapidly emerging hull, one of the first systems to be tested. Based on recovered paint traces, the colorful engine might have been red or green with bright brass steam gauges, wheels, and fittings, and a silver-faced clock. It sat on diamond-patterned floor plates, apparently painted royal blue, and filled the space.

Engineers utilized cramped walkways to gingerly avoid those flashing gears, shafts, and rods, as well as blistery hot pipes, while placing hard tallow in numerous brass oil cups that then dripped lubricating liquid fat into moving parts. Engineer Stimers notified Commodore Smith on December 31 that the engine's performance "was highly satisfactory."

The 120-ton turret soon followed, barged across in sections from Novelty Ironworks in the city and reassembled, the first such mechanism to be mounted on a ship. Smith worried that concussion from gun discharges in the iron cylinder would render men insensible. Ericsson countered that the turret's great weight would absorb vibrations while air pressure would

This captain's cabin in monitor USS *Catskill* was very like the one in *Monitor*. Note the open portlight overhead, the elaborate wood paneling and trim, and the iron watertight door at left. The artwork above the hatch depicts a monitor at sea. Only the captain's (and perhaps the executive officer's) cabin would have been this roomy with his own dining table and a water closet (head) probably behind the door at right. (nhhc)

readily dissipate through the perforated grating nine feet overhead and through the floor gratings underfoot.

Despite the rush, Ericsson did not scrimp on interior embellishments, accoutrements, and gadgets. "Our quarters for eating & sleeping are quite small & will not be *uncomfortably comfortable*," Paymaster Keeler wrote to his wife. Victorian opulence—paid from Ericsson's own purse—adorned the officers' cubby hole staterooms with black walnut paneling, white porcelain washbowls displaying "*Monitor*" in gilt letters, tapestry rugs, soft goat's hair mats, and lace-damask curtains in a blue and white floral pattern.

The ceiling in Keeler's room rested a foot higher than he could reach, about nine feet, which was rare on ships. The bunk was comfortable and "just so long that when my head touches one end, my feet touch the other." Elegant brass sconces with oil lanterns provided some illumination, but unless sunlight shone brightly through the six-inch glass deck light over Keeler's head, he kept a candle burning to read or write.

Similar windows partially illuminated all staterooms and the wardroom dining table. One officer reported viewing fish swimming above the thick glass. In port, they could be opened to admit fresh air. Another compatriot once passed Keeler's mail down to him through the aperture. The deck lights would be covered with iron lids at night and in action.

Heaters fed by boiler steam kept the staterooms warm; floor registers admitted fresh air from intake blowers in the engine room. Louvered doors and short room partitions facilitated circulation but provided little privacy or quiet. Keeler complained to Anna about wardroom messmates spouting Shakespeare, criticizing the opera, theater, or "other places not quite as reputable," and reading aloud *New York Herald* personals interspersed with witticisms. Every word resounded in his cabin "as if they were seated by my elbow."

The crew's berth deck next aft—16 by 25 feet—was utilitarian. Fifty or so men slept in hammocks swinging from the overhead but stowed during the day. Oil lamps provided the only illumination although deck hatches could be opened in port. Storerooms, powder magazine, and shell room bordered the space.

Just 20 feet from Keeler's comfortable cabin, fireman George Geer wrote his wife, Martha: "I have for my desk a water pail turned upside down so you see we have not all the improvements of the age." Apologizing for not writing more, he complained: "I am on the Hammocks, where I cannot sett up strait and can hardly move my arms."

Ericsson's innovations included auxiliary steam engines—an uncommon feature at the time—driving the turret, ventilation blowers, and pumps. A steam condenser provided fresh water. Guns were mounted in customized, low-profile carriages. A cylindrical well in the bow allowed raising and lowering the anchor without exposing crewmen.

The inventor installed the first custom-designed, pressure-flushing, below-the-waterline "water closets" or "heads." Surgeon Daniel Logue suffered the indignity of being blown off the seat by a jet of water when he operated the flushing valves in the wrong order.

January 14, 1862: A nervous Commodore Smith bluntly telegraphed Ericsson that his 100 days had expired, but the vessel had attained its unique shape and was nearing completion. Requested to select a name for his creation, the Swede replied: "The impregnable and aggressive character of this vessel" will convince Rebels that riverbank batteries will no longer bar the advance of Union forces. And, continued Ericsson, potential European rivals will be "startled and admonished" by this new Yankee notion. Downing Street and Lords of the Admiralty might reconsider those ironclads they were building at huge expense. "On these and many similar grounds I propose to name the new battery *Monitor*." It was a warning, hopefully a deterrent, aimed specifically across the Atlantic as well as towards the temporary Southern threat.

Fireman George Geer exchanged compelling letters with his wife Martha about life aboard *Monitor*. Martha worked as a washerwoman, struggling with malnutrition and sadness. (mmp)

One of Ericsson's later monitor's, the USS *Dictator*, is under construction in a shipshed at Delameter Iron Works, New York City, ca. 1862-63. Delameter built *Monitor's* turret and other components. The figure standing at the bow probably is John Ericsson. (loc)

Monitor carried 10 commissioned officers. Gideon Welles selected as commander one of the new generation's "scientific officers," 27-year-veteran Lt. John Lorimer Worden. Worden served between sea tours at the Naval Observatory in Washington, D.C., an institution that became world renowned for scientific breakthroughs in astronomy, meteorology, oceanography, and navigation under the famous U.S. Navy Lieutenant (and later C. S. Navy Commander) Matthew F. Maury.

Worden had been captured the previous year while running secret dispatches to Fort Pickens in Florida, becoming the conflict's first prisoner of war. Confined in Alabama for eight months before being exchanged, he was still ill and weak when the appointment arrived but rushed off to Greenpoint anyway.

"After a hasty examination of [*Monitor*]," Worden wrote to Commodore Smith, "I am induced to believe that she may prove a success." He was quite willing to test her capabilities and promised to "devote whatever of capacity and energy I have to that object." Worden formally assumed command on January 16.

Lieutenant Samuel Dana Greene was named executive officer, second in command. The 22-year-old Marylander graduated from the United States Naval Academy at Annapolis in June 1859. Founded in 1845, the academy kindled a revolution in officer training with academic standards comparable to West Point. Greene represented the young professional officer corps incubated at the new school, steeped in new technologies, and fired in the crucible of war to lead the navy into the twentieth century.

The only other sea officers were two masters—a warrant officer position expert in navigation and piloting. Surgeon Logue and Paymaster Keeler came aboard as staff officers. Four engineers managed the machinery: first assistant through fourth assistant.

First Assistant Engineer Isaac Newton Jr., the most experienced (aside from the unofficial presence of Chief Engineer Stimers), held a civil engineering degree from the University of the City of New York

Monitor crewmen relax on the aft deck in July 1862. The smokestack behind the sailor reading at left center was removable and collapsible for combat but was too short to keep seas out during the trip from New York. Just in front of him, the cover is off the hatch to the engine room. Note removable iron ladder to the turret top. (nhhc)

and a New York State Engineer's Certificate. He had been first assistant engineer aboard the *Merrimac*-class frigate, USS *Roanoke*.

Despite little public notice, a large, spontaneous crowd appeared on the drizzly morning of January 30, 1862, to witness *Monitor's* launch into the East River. John Ericsson stood confidently on deck with a few associates, although a small boat stood by just in case. According to the *New-York Tribune*, "The assemblage cheered rapturously" as the "strange-looking craft glided swiftly and gracefully into its new element." Nearby vessels fired salutes.

The *New York Times* touted the successful launch "notwithstanding the prognostication of many that she would break her back or else swamp. . . ." The *New York World*: "It was very evident to the dullest observer, that the battery had not the slightest intention of sinking." Assistant Navy Secretary Gustavus Fox telegraphed Ericsson: "I congratulate you and trust she will be a success. Hurry her for sea, as the *Merrimack* is nearly ready at Norfolk and we wish to send her there."

Work surged around the clock to complete fitting out. Journalists flocked to Greenpoint and swarmed the ship, leaving in their reporting little to the imagination despite Commodore Smith's futile attempts at secrecy. "The impression prevails here that our destination is the Potomac & our business will be to dust the rebel batteries off its banks," Keeler wrote to Anna. He hoped so; those batteries "have so long disgraced the vicinity of the Capital. If that work is set off to us & we can do it, it will be glory enough."

Captain Worden, choosing not to trust arbitrary assignments of available sailors to complete his crew, sought volunteers from warships in New York harbor. Addressing crews of the 74-gun ship-of-the-line USS *North Carolina* and the sailing frigate USS *Sabine*, Worden described the probable perils of passage and the certainty of combat. Many more men enthusiastically responded than required. "A better [crew] no naval commander ever had the honor to command," he stated in the after-action report.

Fifty-five sailors constituted the crew. Senior enlisted petty officers included a gunner's mate, master's mate, master-at-arms, boatswain's mate, and two quartermasters. Seamen manned the guns and operated and maintained the vessel—anchoring, mooring, and managing boats and supplies. The normal and numerous sail handlers were unnecessary.

Cooks, stewards, and servants performed their duties. Firemen and coal heavers kept steam machinery operating and received higher wages than seamen due to the discomforts involved and shortage of recruits. Worden's nephew, Daniel Toffey, became his clerk.

Although a few of these men had prewar sea service, most arrived as recent recruits. Previous occupations included farmer, machinist, carpenter, stonecutter, sailmaker, store clerk, or "none." Some were immigrants: Scandinavian, German, Austrian, English, Scots, Irish, Welch. At least two were African-American, including one officer's steward.

The USS *Monitor* slides down the ways into the East River in this *Harper's New Monthly* drawing. The size of the shed is exaggerated. (nhhc)

The volunteers endured ribbing from fellow seamen. In a "solemn and prophetic tone," one old salt proclaimed: "You fellows certainly have got a lot of nerve or want to commit suicide, one or the other." Several of them took one look at *Monitor* and promptly deserted.

Enthusiastic ladies visited "in the hundreds," Paymaster Keeler informed his wife, while he had the pleasant duty of showing them around. "You can imagine your polished & accomplished husband *shining* in this new sphere—I believe I got along well enough. I rubbed up my antiquated & somewhat indistinct ideas of etiquette & bright buttons & Shoulder straps made up any deficiency."

Bright buttons, which Keeler enjoyed passing around, "are a sure passport to the notice of the weaker sex. . . . It's real fun—don't get jealous—I thought often of you & our friends at home today & wished you might have been among the gay crowd."

The turret first rotated on February 17. Secretary Welles issued orders to proceed when ready to Hampton Roads. On the 25th, Lieutenant Worden opened the logbook, brought his crew onboard, and read *Monitor* into commission as a third-rate steamer of the United States Navy. It was a cold, clear day. "Everything was hurry & confusion on board expecting to start immediately," wrote

Ironclad Seaman Oscar W. Farenholt strikes a dapper pose in this 1862 Carte de Visite. His hat ribbon identifies him as a crewman aboard the monitor USS Catskill. (nhhc)

Keeler. "Powder, Shot, shell, grape & canister were taken on board in abundance." He had made what he assumed to be his last visit ashore.

Two days later, continued Keeler, the hawsers were cast loose, and they were underway amid a terrible snowstorm. The vessel, however, caromed back and forth across the river between New York and Brooklyn "like a drunken man on a side walk, till we brought up against the gas works with a shock that nearly took us from our feet." A week earlier, *Monitor* had steamed over from Greenpoint to the Brooklyn Navy Yard in smooth water with no serious difficulties, but now in rough conditions, the helmsman could not control the rudder.

Monitor straggled back to the navy yard with the press reporting on "Ericsson's Folly." The chagrined inventor redesigned the rope, block, and tackle mechanism to multiply wheel-to-rudder mechanical advantage. Upon completion, Captain Worden insisted on additional trials off Sandy Hook observed by a board of senior officers and engineers. This delay proved costly to the fleet in Hampton Roads.

The test spin occurred on a dismal, rainy day—March 3. Under 30 pounds of steam, making 50 RPM of the propeller, and with helm hard a starboard, *Monitor* reversed course within three times her length in 4¼ minutes, which was reasonably agile for a big hunk of iron. The much larger and deeper *Virginia* required 30 minutes to turn around.

Monitor's two 13-foot-long, 8-ton Dahlgren smoothbores also were tested, first with blank cartridges, then grape, and finally canister with a full powder charge. Ericsson's gun carriages rested on wrought iron slides and wheels with friction clamps to restrain recoil in the 20-foot space, but the operation of the clamps proved confusing.

During the test, Engineer Stimers managed in both cases to rotate the brass hand wheels in the wrong direction, releasing rather than tightening the friction. Each unrestrained gun leapt back when fired, crashing into the rear turret bulkhead and leaving a sizeable dent but causing no injuries.

Although the gun tests were otherwise successful, Worden was ordered to use only half charges in combat—15 pounds of powder—for fear of bursting the gun in the turret, a decision they would regret. A half charge hurled 187-pound solid shot or 168-pound explosive shell up to 1,700 yards. The engine test also was considered successful, although Stimers and Ericsson could coax only 6 of the planned 9 knots out of her at a maximum 64 RPM.

Bucking thick rain, strong northeast winds, and a powerful ebb tide, *Monitor* returned to the yard. That evening, noted Keeler, a special dinner was held in the wardroom with the senior test observers. Although "suited to the occasion," the meal was rather spoiled by a steward who had been sampling liquid refreshments before serving.

Champagne arrived in brandy glasses and vice versa while the fish was brought in before the soup was finished. "However everything passed off as well as we could make it." The paymaster witnessed "a little more man of war discipline" when the steward was shackled and confined in the chain locker.

At 10:00 p.m., recorded the logbook, "Norman McPherson & John Atkins deserted taking the ships cutter & left for parts unknown. So ends this day." Keeler: "We are finally all ready for a start & are now only waiting for a favorable wind, not to fill our '*billowing*' sails, but to give us smooth water." The storm raging on the coast held *Monitor* in Brooklyn and delayed *Virginia's* sortie from Norfolk for two more days.

A Matter of the First Necessity

CHAPTER FIVE

MAY 1861 – MARCH 7, 1862

If *Monitor* exemplified Yankee ingenuity and industrial prowess, the CSS *Virginia* was the epitome of Confederate naval strategy and execution. The strategy was to counter overwhelming material inferiority with cutting-edge technology. The Rebel warship design was less revolutionary but elegant in simplicity: an iron-encased shed on top of an existing hull and engineering plant.

Virginia launched as the brainchild of innovative, dedicated, and professional men, but was the victim of poor planning and coordination, hurried construction without testing or refinement, and a dearth of critical resources. Still, she was perceived as an existential threat to the Union.

One commodity the South did not lack was senior naval talent, starting with Secretary of the Navy Stephen Russell Mallory, arguably President Jefferson Davis's most capable cabinet officer and one of only two to serve from the Confederacy's first days to its last. Davis, whose talents and interests lay in army affairs, left the navy to Mallory.

John Ericsson acknowledged the "great professional skill" demonstrated in Confederate naval administration. "Indeed, the utility of the armor-plating adopted by France and England proved to be better understood at Richmond than at Washington."

Unlike his Yankee counterpart, Gideon Welles, Mallory had the resume. An experienced and technically knowledgeable maritime lawyer from Key West, Florida, Mallory served through the 1850s as U.S. senator and chairman of the Senate Committee on Naval Affairs where he crusaded for modernization.

Norfolk Navy Yard Drydock Number One in 1933 is little changed since it hosted the *Merrimack* to *Virginia* conversion. This oldest operational drydock in the United States is almost 300 feet long, built of Massachusetts granite. It began service in 1834 and is still used today. (nhhc)

Stephen Russell Mallory (1812-1873), Secretary of the C. S. Navy, espoused technical innovation and what today is termed "asymmetric warfare," as befits the underdog. In addition to ironclads, he sought light, swift commerce raiders and blockade runners while promoting advanced weapons such as "torpedoes" or mines and rifled naval artillery. Mallory and the dedicated men of his navy were more successful in these endeavors than circumstances warranted, contributing to the longevity of the Confederacy.
(nhhc)

Mallory's tenure witnessed epic transformations—sail to steam, paddles to propellers, larger, more powerful artillery, explosive shells and rifled bores. He monitored developments closely and insisted the U.S. Navy keep up with foremost rivals Great Britain and France. He sponsored the *Merrimack* class of frigates.

Senator Mallory enthusiastically advocated iron armor even before the country's fledgling metals industry could supply it in requisite quantities and quality. During another war scare with Great Britain in 1841, Congress approved construction of a steam-powered, ironclad floating battery to defend New York harbor named the Stevens Battery, after its inventor.

Then tensions eased; the project stuttered along until 1853 when it again came before Mallory's committee for funding. Although unsuccessful in the Senate that year, his pleadings for the Stevens Battery presaged his thinking of 1861, when he resigned his seat and followed Florida into the Confederacy.

Now the new secretary, Mallory had to buy and build a navy from scratch to challenge the formidable one he helped develop. "I regard the possession of an iron-armored ship as a matter of the first necessity," he reported to the Congressional Committee on Naval Affairs in May.

However, *Virginia* as she eventually emerged was not what he had in mind. Mallory cited a detailed history of rival French and British programs to justify seagoing ironclads like France's *Gloire*. "Such a vessel at this time could traverse the entire coast of the United States; prevent all blockades, and encounter, with a fair prospect of success, their entire Navy."

The Confederacy had almost no infrastructure, industrial capacity, or experience to build warships. "But inequality of numbers may be compensated by invulnerability; and thus not only does economy but naval success dictate the wisdom and expediency of fighting with iron against wood, without regard to first cost. . . ."

Mallory looked first across the Atlantic for ironclad rams (and for blockade runners and commerce raiders). He dispatched an agent with $2 million appropriated by the Confederate Congress for just such a purchase, perhaps *Gloire* itself. This international business with rebels became a major source of acrimony between Great Britain and the United States.

Not surprisingly, no ironclads were for sale. In March 1862—while *Virginia* terrorized Hampton Roads—

One of the "Laird Rams" is pictured after commissioning in the Royal Navy as the HMS *Wivern*. These innovative vessels severely frightened the Lincoln administration over the threat to the blockade. Note the bulwark sections abreast the two turrets lowered to allow firing of the guns. (nhhc)

Mallory contracted the British firm of Laird & Son near Liverpool to construct two iron-hulled, double-turreted, ram-equipped warships.

But once completed in October 1863, the British government confiscated the fearsome "Laird Rams" after U.S. Secretary of State William Seward threatened war if they were delivered to the Rebels. The impressive ironclad CSS *Stonewall*, built in Bordeaux, France, sailed in March 1865 for the Confederacy but arrived too late.

In that first summer of the war, Mallory had to build ironclads at home, and quickly; he started projects in Memphis and New Orleans as well as Portsmouth. The secretary conferred with Confederate Navy Lt. John Mercer Brooke to develop a feasible ship design. Brooke, a graduate of the Naval Academy class of 1847 and 20-year veteran, was one of the most capable in the new generation of scientific officers to "go south."

Like John Worden, *Monitor's* commanding officer, Brooke had served prewar at the

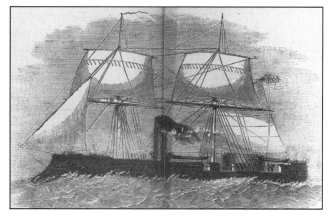

The seagoing ironclad ram CSS *Stonewall* was the Confederacy's last hope for a blockade-busting warship. After crossing the Atlantic to Havana in May 1865, the captain learned of the war's end and abandoned the ship to U. S. authorities. She was sold to the Imperial Japanese Navy (see Foreword). (nhhc)

Washington Naval Observatory as an apt pupil of Matthew Fontaine Maury, the "Pathfinder of the Sea." Brooke invented a new boathook and an effective sounding device for mapping ocean depths; he attained wide recognition as an astronomer/hydrographer surveying the Pacific. He also was the Confederacy's answer to Union ordnance expert John Dahlgren.

Mallory summoned Naval Constructor John Luke Porter and Chief Engineer William Price Williamson for input. Porter had begun the shipbuilding trade in his

John Mercer Brooke, Lt., CSN (1826-1906), was promoted to commander after the Battle of Hampton Roads and in 1863, became Chief of the Bureau of Ordnance and Hydrography until war's end. Brooke became a professor of physics and astronomy at the Virginia Military Institute in Lexington, Virginia, and is buried there in Stonewall Jackson Memorial Cemetery. (nhhc)

father's Portsmouth, Virginia, shipyard. He worked many years in wood, iron, and steam construction—including on *Merrimac*-class frigates *Colorado* and *Roanoke*—but with mixed results.

After failing his first attempt, Porter passed the exam in 1857 for naval constructor (a civilian position like naval architect today) and was employed at the Gosport Navy Yard when it fell to Confederates in April. He was the only naval constructor to join the rebellion. Williamson, a Norfolk native and U.S. Navy veteran, was the Confederacy's senior naval engineer.

Brooke, Porter, and Williamson met with Mallory on June 23. Lieutenant Brooke produced preliminary drawings: "The first idea presenting itself was a shield of timber two feet thick, plated with three inches of iron, inclined to the horizontal plane at the least angle that would permit working the guns."

Constructor Porter brought a model he had created in 1846 for a "flat-bottomed light-draught propeller, casemated battery, with inclined iron sides and ends." The form of the casemate in the two designs was almost identical, but Brooke's had one major difference.

"I proposed having the ends prolonged and shaped like those of any fast vessel," he wrote, "and in order to protect them from the enemy they were to be submerged 2 feet under water, so that nothing was to be seen afloat but the shield itself." The object was to gain speed and buoyancy without exposing the hull or increasing the draft.

This was, according to Mallory, "the peculiar and distinctive feature. . . . It was never before adopted." Still desiring a seaworthy craft and not just a blunt harbor barge, the secretary adopted the lieutenant's concept.

The secretary instructed Porter to prepare working plans for a new construction vessel while Brooke and Williamson sought suitable engines and boilers. But none were to be had; it would take the Confederacy's only capable facility, the Tredegar Iron Works in Richmond, a year to build them.

Meanwhile, the blackened hulk of the former USS *Merrimack* had been laboriously pumped out and towed onto their newly acquired—and only—dry dock at Gosport, one of the finest shipyards in the world. Mallory asked his three advisors to investigate all alternatives.

Their report concluded that *Merrimack*, which was useless for any other purpose, "is our only chance to get a suitable vessel in a short time. . . . The bottom of the hull, boilers, and heavy and costly parts of the engine [were] but little injured." Brooke: "We all thought the draught too great, but that we could not do better." Cost would be about one-third of new construction. The secretary informed Congress he could convert *Merrimack* to an ironclad for $172,523, and the project was approved.

Mallory created a confusing, overlapping chain of responsibilities. As shipyard commandant, Flag Officer French Forrest retained administrative control, but he exhibited little enthusiasm for the project. Naval Constructor Porter supervised hull and casemate work; Chief Engineer Williamson oversaw machinery revitalization; Lieutenant Brooke acquired the armor and armament while acting as the secretary's overseeing agent.

Construction was underway by July 1861, news of which incited Gideon Welles to action, but the Confederacy had a head start in the ironclad business. Porter and Brooke argued publicly about credit for the vessel's design, presaging a difficult relationship.

Porter removed burned portions of the ship, chopped her down to about two feet above the original waterline, and constructed a new gundeck of planks supported by iron beams. Engines and boilers remained in position below the berth deck. Work began on the casemate in August.

"Lieutenant Brooke was constantly proposing alterations," groused Porter, "and as constantly and firmly opposed by myself." Among the changes: Porter designed single fore and aft gun ports; Brooke demanded three ports in each casemate end for pivot guns covering corner blind spots. Porter had two hatches to the casemate top deck; Brooke wanted four so crewmen could repel boarders.

Porter disapproved of the ram concept—an afterthought proposed by Secretary Mallory; Brooke made it happen. Porter left rudder-control chains on the aft deck exposed to shot and shell; Brooke ordered that the chains be sunken into protective iron channels. To the lieutenant, these modifications affected "very materially" the efficiency of the ship, but they caused delays.

Lieutenant Brooke also worried about Porter's armor specifications: three overlapping layers of 1-inch iron plate. Solid iron up to 3 and 4 inches thick had proved superior to laminated plate in European tests. Tredegar Iron Works was not, however, configured to roll and punch large quantities of iron thicker than one inch. Brooke decided to conduct a live test at an isolated site on Jamestown Island in the river below Richmond.

Lieutenant Catesby ap Roger Jones joined him. The 40-year-old Virginia native had been 25 years in the U.S.

John Luke Porter (1813-1893), Naval Constructor, USN and CSN, would continue designing Confederate ironclads in Richmond and later Wilmington. He was promoted to Chief Naval Constructor in January 1864. (nhhc)

Ruins of Norfolk Navy Yard, Portsmouth, Virginia, 1862. (nhhc)

Navy, mostly at sea. He also was a noted ordnance expert who had assisted Lt. John Dahlgren in the 1850s, developing the 9-inch smoothbore shot/shell gun that bore his name and became the navy's standard weapon. Jones supervised testing of the guns when first installed on the new *Merrimack* in 1856. Union Admiral David D. Porter remarked that he only regretted losing two men from the United States Navy: John Brooke and Catesby Jones.

Brooke and Jones manufactured a 12-foot square replica of the planned shield with two feet of oak and pine backing behind the proposed three layers of 1-inch iron, inclined at 30 degrees. Brooke's report: "At a distance of about 300 yards, 8-inch solid shot. . .penetrated the iron and entered 5 inches into the wood; and this was the case with several shots—some seven or eight."

They constructed a new target with two layers of 2-inch plate and fired again with 8-inch shot and 9-inch unloaded shells. "The outer plates were shattered, the inner were cracked, but the wood was not visible through the cracks in the plating." Everyone agreed that she must be clad with 4 inches of iron in 2-inch plates. Brooke later concluded that *Monitor's* 11-inch shot would have "very readily" penetrated the shield as originally designed.

This engraving shows, with inaccuracies, CSS *Virginia* nearing completion in drydock. (nhhc)

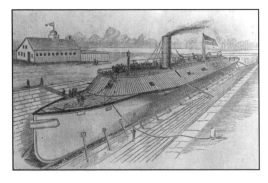

To roll 2-inch plate, Tredegar widened the doors of the annealing furnaces, installed a new waterwheel, and assigned additional workers. The thicker plates could not efficiently be cold punched for bolt holes; they had to be drilled, which cost additional time and money.

First, they had to find iron, another scarce resource. Scouring the Gosport yard produced around

2,000 tons of old tools, useless and obsolete guns, and scrap, but not enough for the ironclad among other requirements. The alternative solution would become frequent but disastrous in the long term: dismantle railroad lines.

Brooke started with the Baltimore & Ohio whose tracks in the lower Shenandoah Valley Stonewall Jackson had torn up. He exploited indefensible Southern lines such as the one from Winchester to Harpers Ferry and cadged surplus rail from the Danville Railroad. Tredegar would be almost solely occupied for six months rolling 732 tons of iron plate.

Transporting the product from Tredegar in Richmond to the shipyard in Portsmouth over poorly maintained and overburdened rail lines caused severe headaches. The army misappropriated cars or whole trains, sometimes leaving piles of plate alongside the tracks. Flag Officer Forrest sent an officer to look for and reload them. Shipments were routed round about through North Carolina over two railroads.

The casemate was ready for sheathing in November, but the last iron was not delivered until February 1862. "We could have rolled them in Norfolk and built four *Merrimacs* in that time had the South understood the importance of a navy at the outbreak of the war," recalled Chief Engineer Ashton Ramsay.

Secretary Mallory also sought the most advanced armament, reporting to the president, "Rifled cannon are unknown to naval warfare; but these guns having attained a range and accuracy beyond any other form of ordnance,

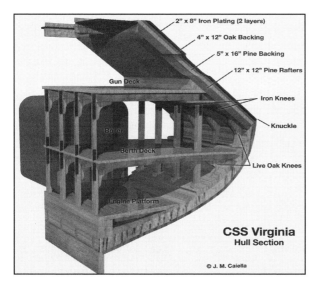

CSS Virginia
Hull Section

© J. M. Caiella

This diagram shows the merging of *Merrimack's* wooden hull with a new gun deck and armored casemate. *Graphic by J. M. Caiella.* (jmc)

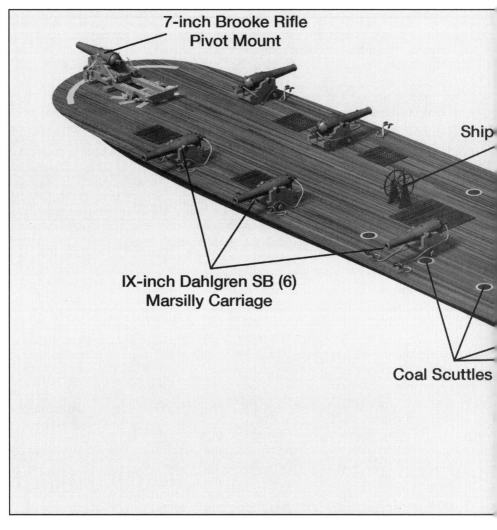

7-inch Brooke Rifle
Pivot Mount

Ship

IX-inch Dahlgren SB (6)
Marsilly Carriage

Coal Scuttles

both with shot and shell, I propose to introduce them into the Navy." John Brooke designed two new rifles: a 7-inch model weighing 15,300 pounds for the fore and aft pivot guns, and a 6.4-inch version weighing 10,675 pounds in broadside.

His innovation was to heat shrink wrought iron bands around the breech for reinforcement against high chamber pressure, and he devised a unique method of rifling. The 7-inch model could throw a 100-pound shell over 4.5 miles with 12 pounds of powder. The Brooke rifle would be one of the South's most deadly heavy artillery pieces afloat and ashore.

The lieutenant also worked on explosive shells and fuses for the rifles, along with a flat-headed, elongated, wrought-iron or steel bolt designed specifically to punch

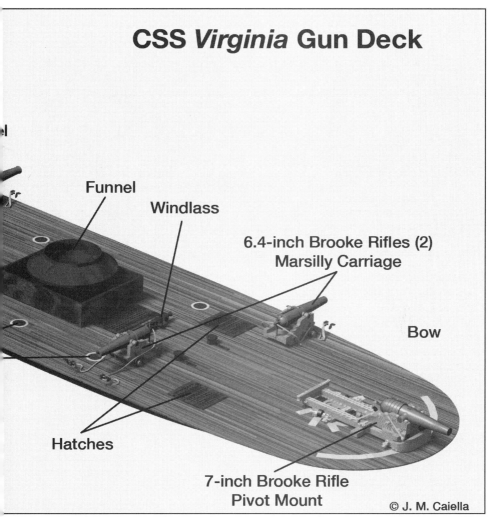

CSS *Virginia* Gun Deck

Funnel

Windlass

6.4-inch Brooke Rifles (2)
Marsilly Carriage

Bow

Hatches

7-inch Brooke Rifle
Pivot Mount

© J. M. Caiella

through iron armor. With such constrained resources—and assuming they initially would be facing wooden warships—he decided to delay production of the armor-piercing bolts in favor of explosive shells, a decision they would regret. Brooke completed the battery with six of the original 9-inch Dahlgren smoothbores from *Merrimack's* stock, modifying two for hot shot.

In November, upon Brooke's recommendation, Secretary Mallory assigned Lt. Catesby Jones as the ironclad's executive officer and second in command. He would facilitate construction, mount the ordnance, and prepare her for sea. He also had to referee conflicts between Brooke and Porter.

But the most pressing task was to assemble officers and crew. For this most prestigious assignment, Jones

Virginia's gundeck mounted two 7-inch Brooke rifles on pivot mounts fore and aft, six IX-inch Dahlgrens, three port and three starboard, and two 6.4-inch Brookes, one port and one starboard. *Graphic by J. M. Caiella.* (jmc)

The Tredegar Iron Works in Richmond (pictured in 1865) was the biggest ironworks in the Confederacy and a significant factor in locating the capital there. Tredegar supplied about half the army's artillery as well as machinery and armor plating for ironclads. The works avoided destruction during the evacuation and continued production through mid-20th century. Tredegar now is a National Historic Landmark and site of the American Civil War Museum. (loc)

could choose from a superlative group of officers, including lieutenants John Taylor Wood, Hunter Davidson, Charles Carrol Simms, and John Randolph Eggleston. Both Wood and Davidson had graduated from and later taught at the Naval Academy. They would be joined by Robert Dabney Minor as flag lieutenant to Flag Officer Buchanan. Minor had assisted Matthew Fontaine Maury with electric torpedo experiments.

A few experienced seamen signed on, those who had deserted or resigned from the U.S. Navy to serve the South, including some petty officers—gunners, boatswain mates, master's mates. Englishman Charles Hasker had been a Royal Navy seaman before immigrating to America.

The army reluctantly and at much urging from Secretary Mallory allowed some transfers. Major General John B. Magruder, commanding the Army of the Peninsula, offered 200 volunteers from his meager force. Captain Thomas Kevill and 39 men from the United Artillery, Company E, 41st Virginia Infantry Regiment—all trained artillerists and many with seafaring backgrounds—volunteered as a body. They manned one of the 9-inch Dahlgrens and filled in on others.

Lieutenant Jones dispatched Lieutenant Wood to personally choose 80 of Magruder's soldiers with seamanship or gunnery backgrounds, but when the group arrived for training, all but two had been switched. "They are certainly a very different class of men from those I selected," Wood reported to Mallory, who then complained to the secretary of war about lack of cooperation and substitution of castoffs. Some arrived chronically ill. Others came aboard in double irons under punishment for insubordination or other infractions.

Jones immediately freed the miscreants saying he would have no forced volunteers. If they chose to remain, they would start fresh. "This course proved eminently judicious, as some of them were the best men on board," recalled Lieutenant Minor. Wood culled additional volunteers for the 320-man crew out of regiments stationed nearby from all over the South. One Virginian listed his prewar occupation as "comedian."

Meanwhile, Chief Engineer Williamson struggled to get the poorly designed, underpowered, and inefficient engines working, a circumstance made worse by fire and emersion. "Great credit is due [to Williamson] for having improved the propeller and engines," wrote Constructor Porter. He increased the speed by three knots. But the engines were still temperamental and, in Lieutenant Jones's opinion, "radically defective."

Lt. Catesby ap R. Jones would be promoted to commander and spend the remainder of the war superintending the vital ordnance works at Selma, Alabama, manufacturing heavy guns. (nhhc)

On January 1, 1862, Mallory detailed Henry Aston Ramsay to the ironclad as her chief engineer. During the last cruises of the USS *Merrimack*, Ramsay had been assistant engineer under Chief Engineer Alban Stimers (who now was busily finishing *Monitor*). Although the Confederacy enjoyed a surfeit of talented line officers, navy engineers were rare. Mallory was fortunate to have Williamson and Ramsay.

By year's end, the *Merrimack* conversion ran almost two months behind schedule with only part of the casemate starboard side sheathed and none of the stern. "The want of interest and energy in completing the Merrimac is disheartening," wrote Lieutenant Jones. At his insistence, boilermakers and machinists were impressed from nearby civilian yards; blacksmiths and finishers agreed to work overtime free of charge. The workforce swarming around the vessel approached 1,500 men.

When an armada of Union warships and troop transports occupied Hampton Roads on January 8, Confederates scrambled to organize invasion defenses, but the fleet departed three days later for North Carolina. Headlines in the February 4 *New York Times* trumpeted *Monitor's* launching in Brooklyn while an issue of *Scientific American* described her construction in exquisite detail. Union capture of Roanoke Island on February 8 threatened Norfolk from the rear, increasing anxiety to complete the ironclad.

"I received but little encouragement from any one," Constructor Porter recalled. "Hundreds, I may say thousands, asserted she would never float." They said she would turn bottom up; she would not steer; behind all that iron, crewmen would suffocate or be deafened by concussion of the guns. "You have no idea what I have suffered in mind since I commenced her, but I knew what I was about, and I persevered," thanks to many sleepless nights and a kind Providence. "I must say I was astonished at the success of the Virginia."

Armor test pieces at the Washington Navy Yard in 1866 display the effects of large projectiles fired at them. (nhhc)

CSS *Virginia* Armament Graphic by J. M. Caiella. (jmc)

On February 17, 1862, by order of Flag Officer Forrest, the converted *Merrimack* was launched and christened the CSS *Virginia*. Marine Pvt. William Cline, stationed in the bow, remembered: "There were no invitations to governors and other distinguished men, no sponsor nor maid of honor, no bottle of wine, no brass band, no blowing of steam whistles, no great crowds to witness this memorable event." Just the workers watched.

Forrest instructed Lieutenant Jones to bring aboard all officers and crewmen with baggage and hammocks. But *Virginia* was far from complete and suffered from one major flaw. As with *Monitor*, the intersection of the vessel's top and bottom structure where shield met hull—the "knuckle"—was a weak point.

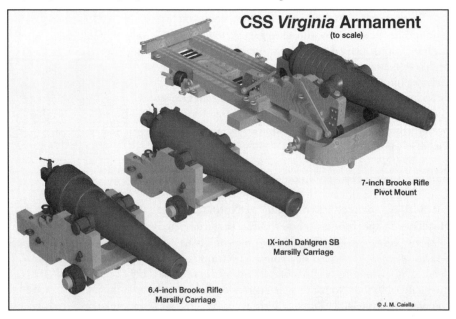

CSS *Virginia* Armament
(to scale)

7-inch Brooke Rifle
Pivot Mount

IX-inch Dahlgren SB
Marsilly Carriage

6.4-inch Brooke Rifle
Marsilly Carriage

© J. M. Caiella

Porter's design placed the knuckle two feet below the surface for protection. He forgot, however, to subtract the weight of the frigate's original masts, rigging, and upper decks when calculating displacement (how deep the ship would sit in the water). *Virginia* floated too high.

"She is not sufficiently protected below the water," Jones reported to Brooke. In smooth water, the knuckle sat six inches immersed rather than two feet; with a slight ripple, it would be wholly exposed. "We are least protected where we most need it. . . ." A 32-pound shot could sink her.

Jones could add additional ballast to the hold, but the increased weight might open seams in the hull. A full load of powder,

shot, shell, and coal would help, but would be expended during battle. "This is a bad piece of work," proclaimed the *Mobile Register.*

Toil continued feverishly on innumerable details. Flag Officer Forrest begged, borrowed, or traded coal and gunpowder from every conceivable source, including powder from Huger's batteries, and still did not obtain a full load. One hundred fifty tons of coal and a thousand pounds of powder helped lower the ironclad in the water. Tredegar had not completed the cast iron gun port shutters, and so they were installed only on the end ports while broadside ports remained uncovered.

Virginia needed a commanding officer. As senior captain, French Forrest campaigned for the position, but Secretary Mallory wanted his most aggressive officer. To circumvent this sensitive issue, Mallory appointed Capt. Franklin Buchanan to the new flag officer position of area naval commander. *Virginia* went into battle without an official captain, but with Buchanan in charge and Executive Officer Lt. Catesby Jones as his second.

Despite *Virginia's* shortcomings, Buchanan would attack. He dispatched Lieutenant Minor to the mouth of the Elizabeth River on March 7 to survey Union fleet dispositions. He returned with an enthusiastic report. "I have great hopes in our success," Minor wrote to his wife. "I reconnoitered the enemy. . .and was glad to be able to report that they were not in such force as I had been led to suppose."

In this stereograph, a 7-inch Brooke rifle on a swivel mount identical to *Virginia's* installation squats in a Confederate battery on the James River near Fort Darling on Drewry's Bluff. This might be a gun removed from the CSS *Jamestown* before she was sunk on May 15, 1862, to obstruct the channel below the fort and deter Union gunboats. (loc)

An unidentified but determined Confederate navy officer glares out of the past. (loc)

She Went Down with Colors Flying

CHAPTER SIX

MARCH 8, 1862 – EARLY AFTERNOON

The CSS *Virginia* emerged from the mouth of the Elizabeth River near 12:30 p.m., Saturday, March 8, 1862, with smoke spouting from the big stack, and accompanied by gunboats *Raleigh* and *Beaufort*. *Beaufort* took a line from the ironclad's port bow to tug her through the river obstructions near Craney Island and around the tight corner into South Channel. She lumbered past Confederate batteries on Sewell's Point into Hampton Roads at the last of the flood tide.

Flag Officer Franklin Buchanan idled *Virginia* for an hour, testing steerage and machinery while scanning Federals from the narrow deck atop the casemate. Four miles north and east across sparkling blue water, Fort Monroe on Old Point Comfort and the battery on Rip-Raps shoals bracketed the channel leading past the entrance of Chesapeake Bay into the Atlantic Ocean.

Septuagenarian Maj. Gen. John E. Wool commanded the Federal Department of Virginia and Fort Monroe with its artillery and infantry garrisons. Including a brigade near Hampton, Virginia, and two regiments of cavalry, Wool had 10,000 men. Fort Monroe mounted 180 heavy artillery pieces with another 10 on the Rip-Raps.

Arrayed under the forts lay a forest of masts, units of the North Atlantic Blockading Squadron, including the formidable *Merrimack*-class steam frigates USS *Minnesota* and USS *Roanoke* (550 men, 40 guns each) and the sailing frigate USS *St. Lawrence* (450 men, 50 guns). A few paddlewheel and propeller gunboats scattered about along with a dozen support craft and tugboats and two French warships observing for Napoleon III.

Fort Monroe west ramparts and moat. *(loc)*

VIRGINIA GETS UNDERWAY— Crowds of well-wishers line the banks as *Virginia* descends the Elizabeth River from the Gosport Shipyard, navigates river obstacles, and emerges into Hampton Roads to face the Union fleet under the ramparts of Fort Monroe. *Virginia* rounds the corner and steams up channel toward Newport News Point. Federal warships scramble after her.

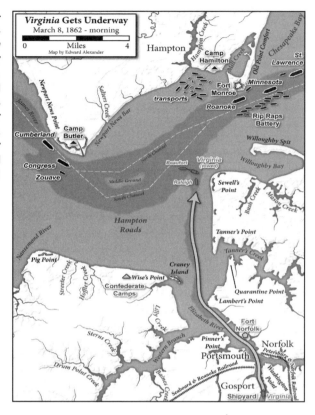

Virginia **Gets Underway**
March 8, 1862 - morning
0   Miles   4
Map by Edward Alexander

A flotilla of 30 to 40 ships and transports, small and large, sail and steam, rested nearby, most of whom would flee *Virginia's* rampage that evening. The paddlewheel gunboat USS *Mount Vernon* spotted the ironclad first, hoisted warning flags, and fired a signal gun. Smoke began to pour from the funnels of *Minnesota* and *Roanoke*, recalled *Virginia* Chief Engineer H. Ashton Ramsay. "Bright-colored signal flags were run up and down the masts of all the ships of the Federal Fleet."

To the west and up channel seven miles, the sailing sloop-of-war USS *Cumberland* (400 men, 24 guns) and the sailing frigate USS *Congress* (480 men, 52 guns) swung lazily at anchor off Camp Butler on Newport News Point attended by the steam tug *Zouave* (2 guns). Brigadier General Joseph K. F. Mansfield commanded the camp with a brigade of 8,000 men in Indiana, Massachusetts, and New York regiments and 8 big cannons.

At daylight that morning, as instructed, Confederate Commander John Tucker's James River squadron— gunboats *Patrick Henry* (12 guns), *Jamestown* (2 guns), and *Teaser* (1 gun)— had come to anchor upriver from Newport News, ready to charge in.

The U.S. Navy deployed in aggregate 2,500 men and over 200 artillery pieces just on the five capital warships. The C. S. Navy brought less than half that number of sailors and 27 guns total on two converted coastal steamers, three puny gunboats, and an ironclad.

Buchanan announced his intentions to *Virginia's* crew and raised the "sink before surrender" signal. He dropped the towline from *Beaufort*, opened steam valves, and chugged straight for *Cumberland* at six knots.

Union Flag Officer Louis M. Goldsborough, commander of the blockading squadron, had been planning this fight at least since the previous October when—based on "minute reliable information"—he reported to Navy Secretary Gideon Welles: "[*Virginia*] will, in all probability, prove to be exceedingly formidable. The supposition of the insurgents is that she will be impregnable."

That same October, General Wool appealed to Commanding Gen. Winfield Scott for the return of four artillery regiments that had been reassigned to defend the capital. He and Goldsborough anticipated a successful assault on Newport News by the Rebel ironclad and her consorts, followed by their escape to sea. Without reinforcements, Wool wrote, "I trust you will not hold me responsible for any disaster that may befall us. . . . The danger, I assure you, is imminent."

The winter of 1861-62 was occupied in constant drill for every contingency, recalled *Cumberland* Lt. Thomas O. Selfridge. "In fact, rumors of [*Virginia's*] expected appearance came so often, that at last it became a standing joke with the ship's company." No fires were allowed. Enforced idleness became "extremely irksome" as they looked forward to spring and active operations.

Looking from the roof of the Hygeia Hotel, the North Atlantic Blockading Squadron is anchored off Old Point Comfort, November 7, 1861. Fort Monroe is at left, mostly out of the picture. The drawing represents the naval expedition under Flag Officer Samuel Francis Du Pont before it departs to capture Port Royal, South Carolina in the first major Union victory. (nhhc)

Joseph King Fenno Mansfield, Brig. Gen., USA (1803-1862) was recommended by General in Chief Winfield Scott for command of the volunteer army being raised in Washington D.C., in spring 1861 but was rejected over concern for his age (57). Mansfield would be given command of the XII Corps two days prior to the Battle of Antietam. On the morning of September 18, 1862, he was shot from his horse leading troops against the Rebel left flank east of the Miller farmstead. (nhhc)

Solid shot had been supplied for *Cumberland's* guns; powder charges had been increased from 10 to 13 pounds, and breeching ropes were doubled to withstand recoil. "One watch slept at the guns, the ship nightly cleared for action, was ready for any emergency."

One of Goldsborough's young sailors, Joseph McDonald of Readville, Massachusetts, recalled serving aboard *Minnesota*: "Her tall sides, pierced for forty-four guns, towering masts and spars, gave her a majestic appearance."

McDonald had voluntarily transferred to the USS *Dragon*, a 92-foot propeller steamer used as a dispatch runner, picket boat, and tug. She mounted one 30-pounder rifle and one 24-pounder smoothbore. "I thought I might get a position as fireman and better pay, and would not have to climb the rigging."

McDonald and his *Dragon* shipmates had known for months that Confederates were "fitting up the old *Merrimac* into some kind of a battery. Every one was guessing as to when she would come out and what she would do, and every ship was held in readiness for the battle sure to come, night or day."

After dark each night, *Dragon* steamed quietly toward Sewell's Point and hovered close to the Rebel fort. "We were always ready to signal the fleet by a rocket if we saw [*Merrimac*] coming, slip our anchor, and run." On one foggy-blind night, they wandered too near. Seeing nothing, but hearing dogs barking close by, *Dragon* beat a hasty retreat before they could be blown out of the water. "We. . .were laughed at by the boys," recalled McDonald.

Periodically, a Confederate truce boat flying a white flag would come out carrying Union sympathizers fleeing north; *Dragon* met them midway. While the officers "with their very formal and dignified manners" transferred passengers and conducted business, the men quietly traded for newspapers, tobacco, etc. Rebels paid handsomely for Boston or New York papers, and had been bragging all spring that their ironclad would soon sink the entire Federal fleet.

Whenever *Virginia* did appear, Flag Officer Goldsborough expected her to head directly toward *Congress* and *Cumberland*. Acutely aware that his most powerful ships might not stand up individually to the ironclad, he planned to let her get well up the narrow channel and then, "put at her" with *Minnesota, Roanoke,* "and everything else," trapping *Virginia* between fires, cutting off retreat, and if possible, pounding her into submission.

Goldsborough was not concerned about *Virginia's* little tenders, *Raleigh* and *Beaufort*. However, "Nothing, I think, but very close work can possibly be of service in accomplishing the destruction of the *Merrimack*, and even of that a great deal may be necessary. From what I gather, boarding is impracticable, as she can only be assailed in that way through her [gun] ports."

For at least a month, *Minnesota* had stood by with steam up, cleared for action. Her Capt. Gershom J. Van Brunt reported to Goldsborough on February 23 that they were "anxiously expecting the long-looked-for Merrimack." She reportedly was out of drydock and a complete success. "We are all ready, and the sooner she gives us the opportunity to test her strength the better." Five days later, he received word that *Virginia* was ready to come out. "I sincerely wish she would. I am quite tired of hearing of her."

Roanoke also was cleared for action, but with a broken propeller shaft, could not get underway on steam power. She blew off steam regularly to deceive the Rebels. *Congress*, *Cumberland*, and *Mount Vernon* were powerfully armed, though with sails only, much less maneuverable even assisted by steam tugs. These were the best the U.S. Navy could send against *Virginia* on March 8.

"I shall never forget that day, nor the next, either," recalled Fireman McDonald. It was bright and clear with no wind, "so the sailing-ships must fight as they lay." About 1:00 p.m. they saw smoke coming down the Elizabeth River. "Pretty soon that great black thing, different from any vessel ever seen before, poked her nose around Sewell's Point and came directly for the two ships." Two small gunboats followed, "just like an old duck and her brood. My, didn't orders ring out sharp, and men jump lively!"

Roanoke and *Minnesota* slipped their anchor cables, hoisted a few sails, and started crawling upstream against the outflowing current pushed by tugboats secured to the sides. "Our gallant tars jumped cheerily to their stations," wrote *Minnesota's* Midshipman Charles S. Cotton to his parents. *St. Lawrence* hoisted her anchor under tow of the gunboat *Cambridge*. Gunboats *Whitehall* and *Mystic* also bore off toward Newport News but would play minor roles.

Coming abreast Sewell's Point, all exchanged fire with shore batteries. "Rebel shot and shell whistled around us like hail stones in a storm," recalled Cotton. One struck the mainmast 15 feet from him, nearly cutting the mast in two, showering him with splinters, and striking a fellow midshipman in the mouth and arm.

John Marston, Capt., USN (1795-1885), became a midshipman during the War of 1812 and would see half a century of service around the globe. (nhhc)

One of the more accurate renderings of the CSS *Virginia* (1898) shows her at anchor in Hampton Roads. (nhhc)

During the Peninsula Campaign, Louis Malesherbes Goldsborough (Captain and acting Flag Officer,) USN, (1805-1877) would refuse to serve directly under Maj. Gen. McClellan. He agreed to "cooperate" but held his ships, including *Monitor*, mostly on the defensive in fear of *Virginia* still prowling the Roads. (nhhc)

It took over an hour for *Virginia* to plod across Hampton Roads as the tide crested at 1:40 p.m. and began to recede. Lieutenant John Taylor Wood, the officer supervising the aft pivot gun, had served on *Cumberland* as a midshipman. He stuck his head out a side port and looked ahead. All was quiet; sails hung loose to dry. "Nothing indicated that we were expected."

Saturday was washing day preparatory to Sunday morning inspections. *Virginia's* Lt. John R. Eggleston saw aboard *Congress* hundreds of uniforms hung on lines stretched in the rigging—white to starboard, blue to port according to custom. "Many a poor fellow who scrubbed his shirt or his trousers, spread on the white deck this morning, shall have no more use for them after their day's work shall have been done."

Eggleston had served as midshipman on both vessels. Since he last saw her, *Cumberland* had been cut down from a two-deck, 50-gun frigate to a single-deck, 30-gun sloop-of-war. "But the *Congress* looked as she did when she was my floating home for nearly three years. Little did I think then that I should ever lift a hand for her destruction."

"The drum and fife are sounding the call to quarters," continued Eggleston. He watched sails furled on *Cumberland* and washing disappear from the rigging on *Congress*. He heard their call to quarters across the water, an exact echo of their own. "We go quietly to our stations, cast loose the guns, and stand ready for the next act in the drama."

A young *Congress* sailor, Frederick H. Curtis, saw black smoke off toward Norfolk. The Rebel ram was coming. The deck was cleared for action. "Every eye on the vessel was on her. Not a word was spoken, and the silence that prevailed was awful. The time seemed hours before she reached us," recalled Curtis.

On *Cumberland*, they also observed commotion in the mouth of the Elizabeth River. The tug *Zouave*, commanded by Acting Master Henry Reaney, received instructions to run down and investigate. She had not gone two miles, reported Reaney, when they saw "what looked like the roof of a very big barn belching forth smoke as from a chimney on fire."

Zouave opened with her forward Parrott rifle, firing six rounds without response (and claiming the first shots at *Virginia*) before *Cumberland* hoisted the recall signal. *Zouave* turned and scuttled back. Lieutenant George U. Morris, *Cumberland's* executive officer, commanded while her captain attended a court martial on *Roanoke* down near Fort Monroe. Morris beat to quarters and cleared for action.

About 2:30, *Virginia* passed *Congress* to starboard and drew within a mile of her first victim. *Cumberland* "was a splendid type of the frigate of the old times, with her towering masts, long yards, and neat man-of-war appearance," wrote Lieutenant Selfridge. The crew "stood at their guns for the last time, cool, grim, silent and determined." These highly trained men were confident in their 80-pound solid shot, "for what was known at that time of the relative merits of iron-clads and wooden ships?"

Crewmen gather on deck of a Union gunboat. Note African Americans by the ship's wheel and seated on the deck apparently sewing at right. The African American standing in front of the wheel wears a petty officer patch (equivalent to corporal or sergeant) on his left sleeve. The man seated left front is a U. S. Marine, as evidenced by his billed cap in contrast to sailors' flat caps. (nara)

The USS *Minnesota* is pictured right center, bows on, in Hampton Roads with other units of the fleet. At right is the USS *Pawnee*, which towed *Cumberland* away from the burning Norfolk Navy Yard. (nhhc)

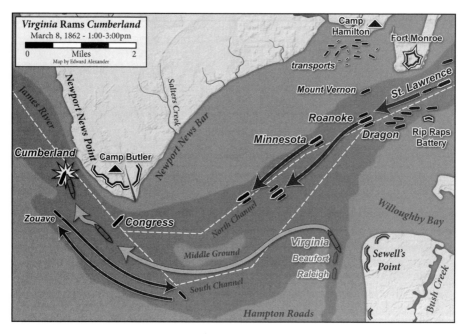

Virginia **R**AMS **C**UMBERLAND— *Virginia* plods across Hampton Roads, exchanging broadsides with the anchored *Congress* as she passes to starboard, and slams into *Cumberland* under the thunderous fire of her point-blank guns. Camp Butler also opens desperate but futile bombardment on the Rebel ironclad. *Minnesota, Roanoke,* and *St. Lawrence* straggle up channel pushed and pulled by steam tugs.

Cumberland mounted eleven 9-inch Dahlgrens per side on the lower gundeck, each with a 16-man crew. On the upper, open deck, a 70-pounder Dahlgren aft and a 10-inch rifle forward, both in pivot mounts, fired to either side. These two powerful weapons particularly worried Buchanan, which is why he went for her first.

Cumberland opened with her forward-most, starboard-side Dahlgrens and the bow pivot, the only guns that could bear as she swung to a single anchor in slack tide. From about 300 yards, *Virginia's* Lt. Charles Simms pointed and fired their bow gun, the 7-inch Brooke rifle maned by 26 gunners. His first shot burst on *Cumberland's* open deck, killing and wounding nine marines.

The second round crashed through *Cumberland's* side at the forward Dahlgren, disabling the gun and destroying the entire crew but the powder man. The gun captain, "a splendid seaman named Kirker," recalled Selfridge, had both arms taken off at the shoulder. As groaning wounded were carried below, it was "an introduction to a scene of carnage unparalleled in war."

"The action soon became general," reported Buchanan, "the *Cumberland, Congress,* gunboats and shore batteries concentrating upon us their heavy fire, which was returned with great spirit and determination." Shells deflected upward, bursting in air, or rolled down hissing into the water, throwing spray into the gun ports.

As *Virginia* neared within a mile of Camp Butler, General Mansfield opened fire with four Columbiads and one 42-pounder James gun. He had three 8-inch siege howitzers hauled over by hand from the land batteries to the riverbank along with two light battery rifles. "It was done with alacrity, and kept up continuously with spirit as long as [*Virginia*] was in range, and although our shot often struck her, they made no impression on her at all."

Lieutenant Eggleston's view on *Virginia*, encased as he was in two and a half feet of wood and iron, was confined to his starboard gun port, some three by four feet. "For a time only the wide waters of the bay and the distant shores were visible, till suddenly the port became the frame of the picture of a great ship."

Congress loomed abeam a hundred yards away, armed mostly with 32-pounder smoothbores. "Suddenly there leaped from her sides the flash of thirty-five guns, and as many shot and shell were hurled against our armor only to be thrown from it high into the air. As by a miracle, no projectile entered into the wide-open ports." *Virginia* returned a four-gun volley.

In 1857, the USS *Cumberland* was cut down (razeed) by removing upper deck guns and lowering bulwarks, lightening the ship and reducing manning requirements. With fewer but newer, larger, and more powerful guns, she was just as deadly. (nhhc)

Frederick Curtis was captain of *Congress* gun number 8 when a Rebel shell struck the gun behind him and detonated, dismounting it, and "sweeping the men about it back into a heap, bruised and bleeding. . . . All I remember about that broadside was of feeling something warm, and the next instant I found myself lying on the deck beside a number of my shipmates. . . . We scrambled to the deck with the expectation that the crew of the 'Merrimac' were about to board us." But she turned toward *Cumberland*.

Down in *Virginia's* engine room, Engineer Ramsay heard two gongs on the bell, the signal to stop, quickly followed by three gongs to reverse. "There was an ominous pause, then a crash, shaking us all off our feet." Lieutenant Eggleston: "Scarcely had the smoke [of the broadside] cleared away when I felt a jar as if the ship had struck ground."

Virginia burst through the heavy anti-torpedo spars floating around *Cumberland's* bow and rammed her almost

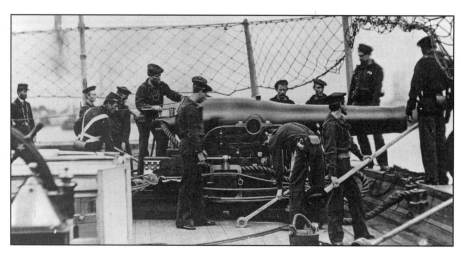

A crew of Union sailors (and one marine with white cartridge belts) mans a IX-inch Dahlgren smoothbore on a slide-pivot mount supervised by an officer at left. From right to left: a sailor holds a long-handled tool, probably a sponge or worm used to remove burning residue from the bore after firing. The long-handled tool at his feet is a rammer for forcing powder bags and shot or shell down the bore. The man behind him holds a large wrench probably used to engage/disengage the pivot rollers under the carriage to adjust aim in train. He has on his belt a cutlass (left), cartridge box (middle), and pistol (right). The next sailor has his left hand on a lever for tightening slide friction pads to dampen recoil. Then a sailor grasps in his right hand the elevation screw lever. He sports a boatswain's pipe lanyard on his chest, marking him as a petty officer and perhaps gun captain. The partially obscured sailor is holding a large iron pry bar used to lever the gun carriage around in train. The marine appears to be tailing onto the block and tackle used to haul the gun forward into battery. The netting is hung to discourage enemy boarders. (nhhc)

at right angles just under the foremast rigging on the starboard side. "The noise of the crashing timbers was distinctly heard above the din of battle," wrote acting captain, Lt. Catesby Jones. "There was no sign of the hole above water. It must have been large, as the ship soon commenced to careen."

The return wave of the collision flooded *Virginia's* forward gun ports. *Cumberland* tumbled heavily to port and began to fill rapidly. Had the officer up near the bow the presence of mind to let go the starboard anchor, wrote Lieutenant Selfridge, "it would have fallen on the Merrimac's deck and she would have been carried down in the iron embrace of the Cumberland. But the opportunity was lost."

Lieutenant Robert D. Minor passed along *Virginia's* gundeck waving his cap, calling out: "We've sunk the *Cumberland*." At his aft pivot gun, Lt. John Taylor Wood recalled: "The blow was hardly perceptible on board. . . . The *Cumberland* continued the fight, though our ram had opened her side wide enough to drive in a horse and cart."

Cumberland let off a broadside just as she was struck. One shell exploded at *Virginia's* bow gun port; fragments tore up the gun carriage, killing two and wounding twelve. Another struck Army Captain Thomas Kevill's loaded Dahlgren, blowing off the muzzle and firing the gun.

Another barrel was lopped off at the trunnions, so short that each subsequent discharge set the wood of the gun port on fire. Crews continued to load and fire the battered weapons— "sponge," "load," "fire!" "[The Yankee's] fire appeared to have been aimed at our ports," noted Jones. "Had it been concentrated at the water-line we would have been seriously hurt, if not sunk."

Virginia's engines labored in reverse, the big propeller thrashed the water, but the two hulls stuck together, recorded Eggleston, like "two mad bullocks with their horns locked." *Cumberland* settled, pushing down and twisting the ironclad's bow. Suddenly, the ram broke off. *Virginia* surged free and swung around, sustaining three point-blank broadsides. "I have often thought since that if the prow had been held fast we would have gone to the bottom with our victim."

"There was a terrible crash in the boiler room," wrote Ramsay. "We thought one of the boilers had burst. No, it was the explosion of a shell in our stack. . . . The firemen had been warned to keep away from the up-take, so the fragments of shell fell harmlessly on the iron floor-plates."

An imprudent sailor stuck his head out a side gun port; a passing shell decapitated him. Two more gunners were killed and five wounded when a Federal shot severed the exposed anchor chain on the bow, causing it to whip inboard. Enemy fire swept away all external appurtenances and riddled the smokestack. They could see *Minnesota*, *Roanoke* and *St. Lawrence* coming up the channel toward them.

Brigadier General R. E. Colston, commanding Confederate forces on the south bank four miles away, watched in amazement. "I could hardly believe my senses when I saw the masts of the *Cumberland* begin to sway wildly." Hordes of civilians and soldiers rushed to the shore to behold the spectacle.

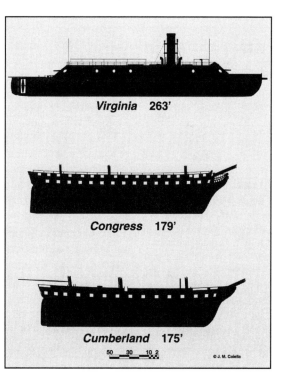

Virginia, Cumberland, Congress comparison
Graphic by J. M. Caiella. (jmc)

"The cannonade was visibly raging with redoubled intensity, but, to our amazement, not a sound was heard." A strong March wind blew directly from them toward the battle. "We could see every flash of the guns and the clouds of white smoke, but not a single report was audible."

On *Cumberland*, "Events followed too fast to record them," recalled Lieutenant Selfridge. The dead were thrown over the side, wounded carried below. "No one flinched, but went on loading and firing, taking the place of some comrade, killed or wounded, as they had been told to do. But the carnage was something awful; great splinters, torn from the side, wounded more men than the shell." He went from gun to gun with a box of cannon primers in his pocket "firing them as fast as the decimated crews could load them."

Cumberland Marine Daniel O'Connor from Staunton, Virginia, wrote home afterwards: "You could hear them cheer [on *Virginia*] but you could not see them. I could hear them laugh, which was aggravating to us in that perdicament." Several men tried to board the Rebel ship, "but it was no go. You could not step on the quarterdeck without walking through blood. Men's legs in one place, arms in another."

Water rose rapidly as *Cumberland* settled by the bows despite frantic efforts at the pumps. According to O'Conner, a *Virginia* officer called over to Lieutenant Morris asking him to surrender, but Morris retorted: "Dam[n] you, you coward you have made a slaughter house of the ship. We will sink with our colors first." "Sink it is," replied the Confederate. Flooding in the forward magazine reached chest high; the men continued passing powder charges up until forced out.

Lieutenant Selfridge would never forget the smoky gundeck covered with dead and wounded, slippery with blood; the galley demolished, its contents scattered; huge guns at all angles, bespattered with gore; rammers and sponges, broken and powder-blacked laying about.

Many wounded had been carried to the berth deck below. "Heart-rending cries could be heard above the

A Currier and Ives lithograph: "The Sinking of the 'Cumberland' by the Iron Clad 'Merrimac', off Newport News, Va., March 8th 1862. 'Cumberland' went down with all her Flags flying: destroyed, but not conquered. Her gallant Commander Lieut. Morris calling to his crew 'Give them a Broadside boys, as she goes'." (nhhc)

A IX-inch Dahlgren rests with Civil War and earlier relics at the Washington Navy Yard, D.C. in 1933. The gun is inscribed: "One of the Guns of the MERRIMAC in the action with the U.S. Frigates CUMBERLAND and CONGRESS March 8th 1862 when the chase was shot off. The mutilation of Trunnions &c shows the ineffectual attempts to destroy the Gun, when the U.S. abandoned the Norfolk Navy Yard, April 20th 1861." This gun now greets visitors at the entrance to the Ironclad Revolution exhibit at the *Monitor* Center. The Parrott gun (second from right behind) is inscribed "Tug Teaser" (see *Teaser* pictures next chapter). (nhhc)

din of the combat, from the poor fellows, as they realized that they were helpless to escape a slow death as the water rose over them."

An exploding shell removed both legs and an arm from a gun captain; the dying man grabbed the firing cord with his remaining hand and fired the gun. "Don't mind me boys, stand by your guns to the last," he said.

"Master-mate Harrington had his head shot off, and fell, a corpse, at my feet," continued Selfridge. "There was no one left in the first division; not a gun's crew could be mustered from the brave fellows who went into action, three-quarters of an hour before, so confident in their ship. . . . They had literally disappeared—died at their posts."

By 3:35 p.m., water poured over the bow as far as the main hatchway. The ship lurched forward and listed heavily to port. The order was passed for every man to look out for himself. Survivors rushed up from below, crowding the ladders. They ran along the deck and piled into boats. Many jumped in and swam or grabbed onto gratings and other flotsam. Some climbed the rigging where they remained until firing ceased.

"The after pivot-gun broke loose and rushed down the decline like a furious animal," recalled Engineer Ramsay, "rolling over a man as it bounded overboard, leaving a mass of mangled flesh on deck."

Another rolling gun knocked Daniel O'Conner down. "I picked myself up as quick as possible & got out the porthole just as the water was commencing." Sitting on the ship's side, the marine removed his coat and shoes, struck out for shore, and was picked up by a boat.

"In this moment of dire confusion with the waters closing over the doomed ship," wrote Lieutenant Selfridge, "the last gun was fired. . . ." It was believed to be gun number 7, fired by Coxswain Matthew C.

George Upham Morris, Lt. USN, (1830-1875) graduated from the Naval Academy in 1852 and retired in 1874 with the rank of commander. (nhhc)

This Leslie's Weekly engraving, ca. 1862, depicts *Cumberland* sailors firing their guns as the ship sinks. (nhhc)

Tierney, who was mortally wounded and perished in the ship. The lieutenant was one of the last to leave the gundeck. The ladders were almost perpendicular.

Selfridge found the ladder blocked by a fat bandsman named Joselyn, struggling up with his drum, who was afterward picked up using it as a buoy. The lieutenant threw off his coat and sword, squeezed through a porthole into the water, and was picked up almost exhausted in a boat with about a hundred men, including Lieutenant Morris. They just shoved clear when the ship went down bow first, stern high in the air, in one plunge.

General Colston: "After one or two lurches, [*Cumberland's*] hull disappeared beneath the water. Most of her brave crew went down with their ship, but not with their colors, for the Union flag still floated defiantly from the masts, which projected obliquely for about half their length above the water after the vessel had settled unevenly upon the river-bottom. This first act of the drama was over in about thirty minutes, but it seemed to me only a moment."

When *Virginia* first appeared, *Cumberland's* commanding officer, Commander William Radford rushed ashore from *Roanoke*, commandeered a horse, and galloped to Newport News only to watch helplessly from the beach as his ship went down. *Cumberland* lost 121 killed and wounded from a crew of 376, including Methodist minister John L. Lenhart, the first U.S. Navy chaplain to lose his life in battle.

Radford reported to Secretary Welles: "No officer or man brought anything on shore save what he stood in. . . . I have the satisfaction of reporting that she was fought as long as her guns were above water. Everyone on board must have done their duty nobly." *Virginia's* Lieutenant Wood concluded: "This action demonstrated for the first time the power and efficiency of the ram as a means of offense. The side of the *Cumberland* was crushed like an egg-shell."

The banner still visible to General Colston was *Cumberland's* long, narrow, warship commissioning pennant streaming from the peak of the mainmast as the hull grounded on sand 50 feet below. Her ensign, flying from the spanker gaff at the stern, went under. As noted by Wood, "she went down with a roar, the colors still flying."

Union soldiers discovered wreckage and collected souvenirs along the shoreline for months. In late May, an army surgeon walking the beach at dusk quietly smoking his pipe came upon a *Cumberland* sailor floating at the water's edge. He pulled the remains up on the sand, covered it with seaweed, and stood by "thinking of the poor nameless thing beneath" until the provost marshal arrived.

"Then, was I homesick?" thought the surgeon. "Only the moon and the stars and the night could testify." A Union nurse observing the warship's protruding masts months later called them a "fit monument—grave and monument as well of heroes."

William Radford, Commander USN (1809-1890). Radford's stepfather, famed explorer William Clark, personally recommended him to President John Q. Adams for a midshipman's berth in 1821. Radford's first service was in the frigate USS *Brandywine* as it returned the Marquis de Lafayette to France. In the battles of Fort Fisher (December 1864/ January 1865), Radford would command the Ironclad Division from his flagship, the USS *New Ironsides*. After the war, he commanded the North Atlantic and European Squadrons and retired as rear admiral in 1870. (nhhc)

John L. Lenhart, Chaplain USN, joined the Chaplain Corps in 1847. (nhhc)

Don't Tell Me Ever Again About Fireworks

CHAPTER SEVEN
MARCH 8, 1862 – LATE AFTERNOON AND EVENING

"Having sunk the *Cumberland*, I turned our attention to the *Congress*," Flag Officer Franklin Buchanan reported. The tide was ebbing and the channel narrow. *Virginia* could not approach her next victim without pushing upstream to a wide, deep spot and turning around. "We were some time in getting our proper position. During all the time her keel was in the mud; of course she moved slowly."

As the cumbersome ironclad swung away from *Cumberland*, they got in a few shots from the aft pivot gun at *Congress*, whose men, thinking the Rebels were retreating, left their guns and gave three cheers. Concluded Buchanan: "They were soon sadly undeceived."

Virginia endured heavy fire from Camp Butler going up and coming back downriver. "We silenced several of the batteries and did much injury on shore," continued Buchanan. The ironclad blew up the transport steamer *Whilden* alongside the wharf, sank one schooner, and captured another. "The loss of life on shore we have no means of ascertaining."

Commander John Tucker's Confederate squadron—*Patrick Henry*, *Jamestown*, and *Teaser*—came charging downriver in line under a full head of steam. Their crews rendered hearty cheers upon witnessing *Cumberland's* demise, recorded *Patrick Henry's* Lt. James H. Rochelle, then braced for "greetings" from Yankees ashore. "And now the hush which precedes the shock of battle settled alike on Federal and Confederate. Glimpses could be caught of the men at their guns through the embrasures of the enemy's batteries, but not a sound came from them."

The USS *Minnesota* cast brass ship's bell is in the collection of the Minnesota Historical Society. (mnhs)

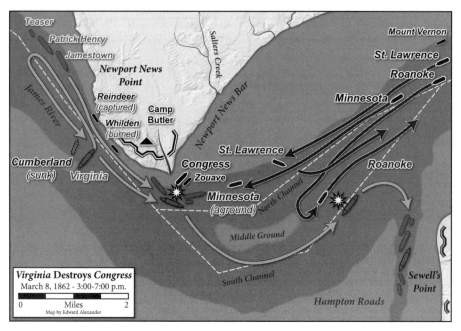

Virginia Destroys Congress
March 8, 1862 - 3:00-7:00 p.m.

0   Miles   2
Map by Edward Alexander

Virginia Destroys Congress— *Virginia* **frees herself from the sinking** *Cumberland***, steams upstream to a wide spot, turns around, and returns to** *Congress***, which has slipped her anchor and been pushed into shallow water by the tug** *Zouave***. The James River Squadron—***Jamestown***,** *Patrick Henry***, and** *Teaser***— charge downstream into the fight.** *Minnesota* **runs hard aground.** *Roanoke* **hits the shallows, but frees herself, turns around and retreats followed by** *St. Lawrence***. With** *Congress* **ablaze,** *Virginia* **and consorts head for anchorage at Sewell's Point. The sun descends as** *Roanoke* **and** *St. Lawrence* **exchange fire with** *Virginia* **and with Confederate batteries on the point.**

The Rebel gunboats ranged abreast those black barrels at 800 yards. "The flash from [*Patrick Henry's*] guns had hardly vanished when the Federal works were wrapped in smoke and their projectiles came hissing through the air," Rochelle continued. Both sides initially overshot their targets, but *Patrick Henry* was struck several times.

One round passed through the crew of No. 3 gun, wounding two and killing one. "Poor fellow, he was an humble hero; his last words as he fell were 'Never mind me, boys'. . . . Whilst the forward guns were engaging one enemy, the after guns were firing at another." Then they focused on *Congress*.

Buchanan's general order required each captain to exercise his own judgment in doing all possible damage. The flag officer subsequently praised their gallant conduct and good judgment in selecting attack positions, and their constant, destructive fire, which "contributed much to the success of the day." He felt sure that the order to sink before surrendering would have been carried out if necessary.

The Union tug *Zouave* found itself in a tight spot, recorded the officer in charge, Master Henry Reaney, between the fires of enemy gunboats and his own shore batteries with shot falling all around. "However, we kept loading and firing as fast as we were able."

Just as *Virginia* reappeared around the sunken *Cumberland*, *Congress* slipped her anchor, loosed her foretopsail, raised her jib, and made signal for *Zouave* to come alongside. With hardly a breath of wind, sails hung useless. Reaney bumped the tug against the frigate's port side while his men clambered aboard to secure lines. "Cries of the wounded were terrible." *Zouave* pushed *Congress* into shoal water where, they hoped, the Rebel ironclad could not ram her.

The USS *Minnesota*, still straggling up to join the action, struck bottom at 3:00 p.m. on Middle Ground shoals. "We immediately backed our engine, but all attempts at getting her off were in vain; for we were hard and fast in the mud," wrote Midshipman Charles S. Cotton. They brought their longest-range guns, a 10-inch pivot and two 9-inch shell guns, to bear on the enemy a long mile away.

"The lofty frigate, towering above the water, now offered an easy target to the rifled guns of the *Merrimac* and the lighter artillery of the gunboats," noted Brig. Gen. R. E. Colston from his vantage point on the south shore. In the shallows, *Minnesota* could not be rammed but she also could not get closer to *Congress*.

Virginia achieved station 200 yards astern of *Congress*, pouring in broadsides while her consorts pounded the Federal frigate. "Our two stern guns were now our only means of defense," wrote *Congress's* executive officer, Lt. Austin Pendergrast. "These were soon disabled, one being dismounted and the other having its muzzle knocked away.

"The men were swept away from them with great rapidity and slaughter by the terrible fire of the enemy. . . ." *Virginia's* hot shot started fires in the wardroom, sick bay, and main hold. One round passed down a line of powder passers, cutting the men down, exploding the powder buckets, and setting more fires. Crewmen manned the pumps, fought the flames, and flooded the magazine.

Gun captain Frederick Curtis recalled: "It was a pretty busy time aboard just then, and the men were much excited. Our little powder boy, a lad of only thirteen years of age, would bring us ammunition, with the tears streaming down his cheeks. He had pure grit and stuck to his duties like a man.

"The order was then passed for us to cease firing, and our colors were struck. My gun was loaded at the time, and, although the order had been given to cease firing, I pulled the lanyard and fired what proved to be the last shot ever fired on board the fated 'Congress.'"

Virginia's Lt. Catesby Jones noted the havoc aboard the flaming frigate. "Her gallant commander, Lt. Joseph B. Smith, was struck in the breast by the fragment of a shell and instantly killed. The carnage was frightful. Nothing remained but to strike their colors, which they did."

As gloom settled over the scene, Curtis picked up one of his gun crewmen with a foot shot off and helped carry him below. "His wounds were fatal, and he died soon after. The sight in the cockpit was an awful one. Wounded and dead were lying all around, and cries of anguish filled the air." Another shipmate was rowed ashore with severe burns on his head and back. "His injuries were fatal, and I helped bury him in the sand the next day."

Returning to the main deck, Curtis encountered an officer who "was very much excited and had his sword in his hand." His last name was Buchanan, brother to the Confederate commander.

Crewmen lowered and scrambled into surviving boats. When Rebels began firing muskets at the boats, recalled Curtis, "The coxswain of one of the boats stood up in the stern sheets and waved his hands at them derisively, for which act he was heartily cheered by those on board the 'Congress.'"

The tug *Zouave* was still secured to the doomed frigate's side. "Blood was running from the *Congress* scuppers on to our deck, like water on a wash-deck morning," wrote Reaney. The tug was taking hits near the engine. The pilothouse and deck were shattered; the figurehead was blown away, and men were down.

Reaney received permission from Lieutenant Pendergrast to cast off and escape if he could. He cut the lines, backed off, and immediately commenced firing at his tormentors. As *Zouave* headed over to assist *Minnesota*, a friendly shell destroyed the rudder post and blew a blade off the propeller, putting her out of action. Reaney believed that *Congress* would have been captured without the tug's assistance.

General Colston observed through field glasses: "Projectiles hurled at the *Merrimac* glanced harmlessly from her iron-covered roof, while her rifled guns raked the *Congress* from end to end. . . . The latter replied gallantly. . .her decks were reeking with slaughter. Then her colors were hauled down and white flags appeared at the gaff and mainmast."

Buchanan ceased fire, climbed atop *Virginia's* casemate, and hailed over to Lt. William Parker commanding *Beaufort*, instructing him to take possession of *Congress*, secure officers as prisoners, allow crewmen to escape ashore, and burn the ship. *Beaufort* and *Raleigh* ran along opposite sides of *Congress* while *Teaser* provided cover.

Accompanied by armed sailors, Parker scrambled aboard the battered vessel where he saw the bloody remains of the commanding officer. He and Lieutenant Smith had been Annapolis classmates, close friends, and messmates on more than one long sea cruise. Gunner Curtis observed the Rebel officer, considering him a brave man. "He was smoking a cigar and seemed to be very cool. When he saw what havoc the shots from the 'Merrimac' had done on board, he said: 'My God, this is terrible. I wish this war was over.'"

"With us of the navy it was real civil war," noted *Virginia's* Lt. John Eggleston. "On both sides we were fighting men with whom we had lately intimately associated in a common profession. We all knew one another personally or by reputation."

Flag Officer Buchanan's brother was a paymaster assigned to *Congress*. Two *Virginia* lieutenants each had a brother and another had a father in the United States Army. A midshipman's father served in the U.S. Navy. Parker sent Smith's sword under flag of truce to his friend's father, Commodore Joseph Smith of the Ironclad Board. *Congress* suffered 121 killed and wounded from a crew of 434 (28%).

This illustration, published in 1907, is titled "Virginia returning to Hampton Roads from James River to attack Congress." Camp Butler batteries blast away in the distance while a Union transport burns, and *Cumberland's* **masts protrude above the waters.** *Virginia* **is inaccurately depicted with pilot houses on both ends of the casemate. Lt. Brooke wanted two but was able to install only the forward one.** (nhhc)

Parker accepted surrender from Lieutenant Pendergrast with his colors, sword, and sidearm. "Some of the rebels acted like crazy men," wrote Curtis, "and would drive our men about like cattle. They became so abusive that one of our men, a darky, shot one of them. I did not think much of such treatment, and went below." The remaining officers and about 20 crewmen delivered themselves as prisoners on board *Beaufort*, but then urgently requested to re-board *Congress* and assist in removing the wounded. They never returned.

Brigadier General Joseph Mansfield watched intently from his Camp Butler fortifications. He ordered Colonel Brown, 20th Indiana, to send rifle companies A and K to the beach along with two rifled guns under Captain Howard. A Dahlgren howitzer manned by a warrant officer and 14 sailors already ashore from *Cumberland* also went into action from an enfilade position covered by sand banks and trees. "We here had them at about 800 yards to advantage," reported Mansfield.

Blistering musket and cannon fire compelled *Beaufort* and *Raleigh* to cast off and back out of range. Two *Raleigh* officers were killed while assisting the wounded along with several Union men. "It became so hot," recorded *Raleigh's* Lieutenant Wood, "that the gun-boats were obliged to haul off with only thirty prisoners, leaving Lieutenant Pendergrast and most of his crew on board, and they all afterward escaped to the shore by swimming or in small boats." Lieutenant Parker had no opportunity to set destructive fires below deck as ordered.

This Union battery at Yorktown, Virginia, resembles the installations at Camp Butler on Newport News Point. (loc)

Flag Officer Buchanan observed anxiously from his perch atop *Virginia*, expecting to see smoke billowing from *Congress's* hatches, but none appeared. "During this delay," he wrote, "we were still subjected to the heavy fire from the batteries, which was always promptly returned."

Anticipating arrival of *Minnesota*, *Roanoke*, and *St. Lawrence*, Buchanan was determined that the helpless frigate should not be recovered by the enemy. "Had she been retaken," noted Lieutenant Jones, "it might have been said that the Flag-Officer permitted it, knowing that his brother was an officer of that vessel."

"That ship must be burned," Buchanan barked to his flag lieutenant, Robert Minor, who promptly volunteered to take a boat under a white flag and set her fully ablaze, again covered by *Teaser*. Buchanan hailed Commander Tucker in *Patrick Henry* and directed him to assist in the destruction. Tucker maneuvered his ship as close as possible in shoal water and readied boats with combustible material.

"This movement of the *Patrick Henry* placed her in the most imminent peril," recalled Lieutenant Rochelle. "She was brought under the continuous fire of three points." On her port quarter were the batteries of Newport News, on her port bow were the field batteries and sharpshooters on the beach, and on her starboard bow was *Minnesota*. "No wooden vessel could long float under such a fire."

Several rounds struck *Patrick Henry's* hull. One blasted a chunk out of the engine's walking beam.

The CSS *Patrick Henry* was built in New York City in 1859 as the steamer *Yorktown*. She carried passengers and freight between Richmond and New York until Confederates seized her on the James River in June 1861. *Patrick Henry* would become a floating Confederate Naval Academy at Drewry's Bluff and was burned upon evacuation of Richmond. During the government's flight to Danville, *Patrick Henry's* midshipmen guarded the treasury, then were given $40 gold each and sent home. (nhhc)

John Randolph Tucker, Commander CSN, (1812-1883) was a commander in the United States Navy, became a captain in the Confederate States Navy, and as a postwar rear admiral in the Peruvian Navy, explored and helped map the upper Amazon Basin. Tucker commanded the ironclad CSS *Chicora* in January 1863 when it attacked Union blockaders off Charleston Harbor. As W. T. Sherman enveloped Charleston, Tucker scuttled his vessels and formed a marine brigade with which he surrendered at the Battle of Sailor's Creek near Appomattox, April 6, 1865.
(nhhc)

Rochelle recounted the words of a gunner at the aft pivot gun. While frantically extracting burning residue from the bore with a long-handled sponge, another enemy projectile neatly lopped off the handle he held, missing him by inches. "Half in prayer and half in despair at being unable to perform his duty, the sponger exclaimed, 'O Lord, how is the gun to be sponged!'"

A shot from either the field batteries ashore or from *Minnesota* blasted through *Patrick Henry's* boiler. Engine and fire rooms filled with steam, scalding five or six firemen to death. The engineers were driven upon deck, and the engine stopped. Seeing the ship enveloped in a cloud of vapor, Federals increased fire. "At the moment no one knew what had happened," continued Rochelle. They thought the boiler had exploded. "It is an unmistakable evidence of the courage and discipline of the crew that the fire from the vessel did not slacken. . . ."

Patrick Henry drifted toward the enemy. Crewmen hoisted the jib sail to force her head around while *Jamestown* ran in and towed her out of danger. The engineers fixed one boiler—the other was out of commission—and she returned to the conflict. Buchanan called the squadron's escape miraculous. "They were under a galling fire of solid shot, shell, grape, and canister, a number of which passed through the vessels without doing any serious injury."

On *Congress*, Curtis found a line hanging out a lower deck gun port, swung out, and dropped into the water. "I sank well under, and on rising to the surface picked up my hat and started for the shore." The water was filled with men. "I saw several of my comrades drown, but was powerless to help them." He swam nearly a half mile and crawled ashore, "so weak that I was hardly able to stand." Camp Butler soldiers provided clothing and food to survivors.

Meanwhile, Lieutenant Minor's boat with white flag flying had scarcely rowed within 50 yards of *Congress* when deadly fire hit them, wounding Minor severely in the stomach along with several of his men, one of whom had an eye shot out. Confederates believed that the boat had been fired on not just from shore but also from *Congress*, which still flew her surrender banners.

Lieutenant Eggleston: "Buchanan, in a ringing voice I can never forget, called down the hatchway under which I was standing: 'Destroy that ------ ship! She's firing on our white flag!' It was even so, incredible as it may seem. . . . Dearly did they pay for their

unparalleled treachery. We raked her fore and aft with hot shot and shell, till out of pity we stopped without waiting for orders." The lieutenant supervised two of *Virginia's* 9-inch Dahlgrens fitted for firing hot shot, one each side amidships.

Two boiler furnaces were used for hot shot, wrote Engineer Ramsay. "They were rolled into the flames on a grating, rolled out into iron buckets, hoisted to the gun-deck, and rolled into the barrel, which had been prepared with wads of wet hemp. Then the gun would be touched off quickly and the shot sent on its errand of destruction."

Union witnesses contended that *Virginia* fired on helpless crewmen in boats attempting to flee the flaming hulk. Lieutenant Jones denied it: They shot primarily at shore batteries or at times aimed "a distant and unsatisfactory fire" at *Minnesota*. And, they employed anti-personnel rounds—canister or grape—only occasionally in reply to musketry from the beach, "which had become annoying."

Still standing in full view atop *Virginia's* narrow casemate, the enraged Buchanan grabbed a musket and joined the fray, plugging away at blue-coated officers ashore. A rifle ball struck him in the thigh. As the flag officer was carried below, he devolved command upon his executive officer, Lieutenant Jones, "with orders to fight her as long as the men could stand to their guns." *Congress* blazed fore and aft.

The USS *Minnesota* led the army-navy expedition that captured Hatteras Inlet in August 1861 and then became flagship of the North Atlantic Blockading Squadron for Flag Officer Goldsborough, although he was absent in March 1862 with Burnside in North Carolina. While anchored off Newport News on 9 April 1864, *Minnesota* would be attacked by the Confederate torpedo boat *Squib*. The spar torpedo charge exploded alongside without causing damage while *Squib* escaped. *Minnesota* also laid down devastating barrages at the Battles of Fort Fisher, December 1864-January 1865, and contributed 240 crewmen to the marine brigade that famously attacked the citadel's northeast bastion with many casualties. (nhhc)

Charles S. Cotton, Midshipman USN would command a cruiser during the Spanish American War and retire as rear admiral. (nhhc)

"A pretty good day's work," Lieutenant Eggleston remarked to Jones. "Yes," came his reply, "but it is not over. The *Minnesota*, the *Roanoke* and the *St. Lawrence* are on the way up to engage us." (Eggleston assumed Buchanan had been felled by a sharpshooter on shore, but years later, he heard that a former Federal marine in *Congress* boasted of having fired the shot while under the white flag.)

Captain John Marston struggled up the channel in *Roanoke* pushed by tugs. "Ten minutes before 4 o'clock we had the mortification of seeing [*Congress*] haul down her flag. I continued to stand on till we found ourselves in 3½ fathoms water and was on the ground astern." He could proceed no farther and made a great target.

Marston had the tug tow his ship's head around until pointed back down the bay and free of the mud. He spread her sails, retreating with the outflowing tide toward Old Point Comfort. *Mystic* and *St. Lawrence* followed while their tugs went to aid *Minnesota*. As the Federal warships retraced their course, Confederate batteries at Sewell's Point opened up.

"Just at that moment the scene was one of unsurpassed magnificence," observed General Colston. "The bright afternoon sun shone upon the glancing waters. The fortifications of Newport News were seen swarming with soldiers, now idle spectators of a conflict far beyond the range of their batteries, and the flames were just bursting from the abandoned *Congress*. The stranded *Minnesota* seemed a huge monster at bay, surrounded by the *Merrimac* and the gun-boats.

"The entire horizon was lighted up by the continual flashes of the artillery of these combatants, the broadsides of the *Roanoke* and *St. Lawrence* and the Sewell's Point batteries; clouds of white smoke rose in spiral columns to the skies, illumined by the evening sunlight, while land and water seemed to tremble under the thunders of the cannonade.

"The *Minnesota* was now in a desperate situation." A large shot hole appeared in her side; fires burned on her decks. "Her destruction or surrender seemed inevitable, since all efforts to get her afloat had failed."

"It was now 5 o'clock, nearly two hours of daylight, and the *Minnesota* only remained," wrote *Virginia's* Lieutenant Wood. "She was aground and at our mercy." But with an ebbing tide and descending dusk, the pilots would not approach the mudbank. Lieutenant Jones decided to withdraw, a decision for which he would be condemned by countrymen.

Virginia exchanged passing shots with *Minnesota* and *St. Lawrence* on the other side of Middle Ground shoals. "The latter frigate fired at us by broadsides," recalled Lieutenant Jones. "Not a bad plan for small calibres against iron-clads, if concentrated. It was too dark to aim well." On their way back across the bay, *Virginia's* officers gathered about the stateroom where their wounded flag officer lay. In a voice filled with emotion, Buchanan said: "My brother, Paymaster Buchanan, was on board the *Congress*."

Virginia and squadron anchored off Sewell's Point about 7:00 p.m. and an impromptu reunion convened on the ironclad. Lieutenant Eggleston noted that the uniform of *Teaser's* Lieutenant Webb was riddled by Minié balls. Near midnight, they finally had supper, the only meal since 8:00 a.m. They watched *Congress* burn.

Meanwhile, Frederick Curtis bedded down with the 5th Indiana at Camp Butler. "There was not much more sleep in that camp that night, and it was a long and dreary night to us." General Magruder was said to be marching down from Yorktown with 10,000 men. Given *Virginia's* assistance, "we did not see what could prevent the place from falling into the hands of the rebels." Cheering was heard from *Minnesota* soon after midnight. They assumed she had gotten afloat again but discovered in the morning that *Monitor* had arrived.

"And now followed one of the grandest episodes of this splendid yet somber drama," continued General Colston. "The moon in her second quarter was just rising over the waters, but her silvery light was soon paled by the conflagration of the *Congress*, whose glare was reflected in the river."

The burning frigate was four miles away but seemed much nearer. As flames crept up the rigging, "every mast, spar, and rope glittered against the dark sky in dazzling lines of fire." Upon the hull's black surface, "each port-hole seemed the mouth of a fiery furnace."

Flames raged for hours. Loaded guns and shells randomly detonated sending forth deep reverberations; one shot sank a small schooner nearby. Masts and rigging still stood, apparently intact, until about 12:30 a.m. when, "a monstrous sheaf of flame rose from the vessel to an immense height.

"A deep report announced the explosion of the ship's powder-magazine." The rigging vaporized. The hull seemed hardly shattered, although several gun ports were blown into single gaps. "It continued to burn until the brightness of its blaze was effaced by the morning sun."

Joseph B. Smith, Lt. USN (1826 - 1862) was the son of Commodore Joseph Smith of the Ironclad Board. He graduated with the Naval Academy class of 1847. Smith served on the USS *Merrimack* prewar and was first lieutenant and acting commander of *Congress* on March 8, 1862. (nhhc)

Congress **blazes as crewmen swim ashore in this 1892 painting by renowned marine artist J.O. Davidson.** *Virginia* **is visible in right background.**
(nhhc)

A Confederate artillery captain observed from Sewell's Point batteries:

The slaughter must have been awful. It was a long way the grandest sight I ever saw. The [Roanoke's] broadside at the 'Merrimac' after dark was grand, but the 'Congress' on fire was sublime. She presented the appearance of a red-hot fire coal chiseled into the shape of a vessel—her masts & hull were all red hot at the same time.

When she exploded, it sounded as if all the guns in his section had been discharged simultaneously. "The column of flame seemed to go up a 1000 ft high," the artillerist said.

Virginia's Engineer Ramsay recalled, "The burning hulk burst asunder and melted into the waters, while the calm night spread her sable mantle over Hampton Roads." In a letter to his family, a young *Minnesota* sailor concluded: "Don't tell me ever again about fireworks."

Union General Mansfield's Newport News batteries and riflemen had been under arms the entire day. None of his command were killed but a private of the 7th New York had his leg taken off by a *Virginia* shell. Another artilleryman had the bones of his foot crushed by a recoiling gun carriage.

The navy's losses must have been great, concluded Mansfield, "although our best efforts were made to save them. Our ships were perfectly helpless against the *Merrimack*, as their broadsides produced no material effect on her."

"Our loss is 2 killed and 19 wounded," reported Flag Officer Buchanan. "The stem is twisted and the ship leaks. We have lost the prow [ram], starboard anchor, and all the boats. The armor is somewhat damaged; the steam pipe and smokestack both riddled; the muzzles of two of the guns shot away. It was not easy to keep a flag flying. The flagstaffs were repeatedly shot away. The colors were hoisted to the smokestack and several times cut down from it.

"The bearing of the men was all that could be desired; their enthusiasm could scarcely be restrained. During the action they cheered again and again. Their

This typical propeller harbor tug, the USS *Zeta*, probably in the James River in 1864-65, closely resembles both the USS *Zouave* and the CSS *Teaser* without guns. (nhhc)

The steam tug gunboat CSS *Teaser* was captured in the James River by the USS *Maratanza* on July 4, 1862 and photographed. This shot of her bow shows the 12-pounder rifled cannon. Note the rammer resting on the carriage slide. (loc)

coolness and skill were the more remarkable from the fact that the great majority of them were under fire for the first time. They were strangers to each other and to the officers, and had but a few days' instruction in the management of the great guns. To the skill and example of the officers is this result in no small degree attributable."

Virginia had been the focus of at least a hundred heavy guns, afloat and ashore, noted Lieutenant Wood. One officer counted 98 indentations in the armor while "nothing outside escaped." Railings, stanchions, boats, and boat davits were swept clean. The flagstaff was finally replaced with a boarding pike.

"After making preparations for the next day's fight, we slept at our guns, dreaming of other victories in the morning." Flag Officer Buchanan and Lieutenant Minor along with other wounded and the dead were landed at Sewell's Point for transfer to the naval hospital in Norfolk.

About 11:00 p.m., one of *Virginia's* pilots glanced toward *Congress*, wrote Lieutenant Jones, "when there passed a strange looking craft, brought out in bold relief by the brilliant light of the burning ship, which he at once proclaimed to be the Ericsson [*Monitor*]. We were

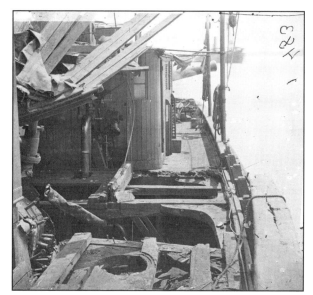

View of damage after *Teaser's* capture showing portions of the steam engine in the splintered deckhouse and the gun barrel of a 6.4-inch rifle on aft deck. (loc)

therefore not surprised in the morning to see the *Monitor* at anchor near the *Minnesota*."

From his headquarters in Fort Monroe that evening, General Wool telegraphed bare facts to Secretary of War Edwin Stanton: *Cumberland* sunk. *Congress* surrendered. *Minnesota* aground; Captain Marston believed she would be taken in the morning. *Roanoke* anchored under the fort's guns. Concluded the general: "It is thought the *Merrimack*, *Jamestown*, and *Yorktown* will pass the fort to-night." Going where, he did not speculate.

The Most Frightened Man

CHAPTER EIGHT

MARCH 8 – 9, 1862

"The house is as full of shadows to-day as if it were haunted by all the ghosts of its long history," recorded presidential secretary William O. Stoddard on Saturday evening, March 8, "but one has just arrived which is altogether new and startling." They received news from Hampton Roads.

White House shadows prominently included Abraham Lincoln's 11-year-old son Willie who died just a fortnight before. The president briefly laid aside his burdens of office—"almost a breaking-down with grief"—but the voice of duty prevailed and "really there will have been no perceptible intermission in the grim routine of the toil which is wearing out the life of Mr. Lincoln."

The frustrated commander-in-chief had convened another council of war that morning to prod Maj. Gen. George B. McClellan into action. McClellan proposed to transport the Army of the Potomac down the Chesapeake and up the Rappahannock River to the Virginia town of Urbanna, outflank Confederate forces near Manassas, and surge 50 miles overland to capture Richmond and end the war. As usual, he proceeded at a glacial pace. "The President is vehemently urging an advance upon Richmond" by any route, wrote Stoddard.

Telegrams filtered in through the afternoon. "The *Merrimack* is being towed down. . .past Craney Island. . . ." "The *Merrimack* is close at hand." "The *Merrimack* is engaging the *Cumberland* at close quarters." "The *Congress* is now burning." And so on. Secretary of War Edwin M. Stanton ordered the news be made public at once to alert Northern merchants that they faced great danger. "For a

A monument to John Ericsson, dedicated in 1926, sits along the Potomac River in Washington, D.C., within sight of the Lincoln Memorial. (loc)

while the news looked very badly," reported another of Lincoln's secretaries, John Hay.

This meant, continued Stoddard, that the James River was closed to Union vessels and troops. "Some of our best ships have been shattered and sunk near its mouth by an iron-armored monster against whose sides their bullets rattled like so many peas. . . ." There was no telling how much more mischief she might do. "Have similar sea-monsters been building in the other rivers and harbors of the Confederacy? . . . The air and the minds of men teem with panicky imaginations hatched out into rumors."

After a long day, they faced a long, dark night. Stoddard wrote: "The hours go by at the White House under the pressure of a constant stream of dispatches, sent over from the War and Navy Departments, except when the President is there himself to read them as they come."

Sunday morning, wrote senior treasury official Lucius E. Chittenden, "was as gloomy as any that Washington had experienced since the beginning of the war. There was no excitement, but all seemed to be overwhelmed with despondency and vague apprehension."

In this view of the White House (1858), President Lincoln's office is behind the south porch on the second floor of the east wing. Here he conducted most business, meeting with the cabinet, answering correspondence, and receiving many visitors. Windows overlooked the stub of the unfinished Washington Monument, the Potomac River, and encampments of Union soldiers. (loc)

John Hay reported panic at Willard's Hotel: "Nothing was too wild to be believed in the way of theory and suggestion." One old gentleman turned purple with fright contemplating the fate of his navy son with General Ambrose Burnside's expedition in North Carolina.

Navy Secretary Gideon Welles arrived at his office early that morning and was examining dispatches when the assistant secretary of war barged in waving a copy of General Wool's final telegram summarizing the dire situation as of Saturday evening. President Lincoln had called an emergency cabinet session at the White House.

Welles scurried over to find Secretary of War Stanton, Secretary of State William H. Seward, and Secretary of the Treasury Salmon P. Chase already with the president "discussing the intelligence in much alarm." They inquired of the navy secretary what could be done to counter this formidable monster. They expected her to wreak still greater havoc, "probably, while we were in council," noted Welles. Others arrived as they talked.

In their Lincoln biography, secretaries John Hay and John Nicolay characterized this cabinet meeting as "perhaps the most excited and impressive of the whole war." Welles also recorded his diary observations in customarily frank, if rather self-absorbed, detail covering intense exchanges throughout the day and evening.

Of the cabinet, only Postmaster General Montgomery Blair was absent. Discussions included General McClellan, Brig. Gen. Montgomery C. Meigs (Quartermaster General of the Army), and Navy Lt. (later Rear Admiral) John A. Dahlgren (Acting Commandant of the Washington Navy Yard).

The Monitor's success would clear the way for Maj. Gen. George B. McClellan's plans for a landing in the James Peninsula. (loc)

"That day and its incidents were among the most unpleasant and uncomfortable of my life," wrote Welles. "The events were momentous and portentous to the nation—the responsibility of it and its consequence were heavier on me than on any other individual—there was no one to encourage and support me."

But his department must meet the emergency. Despite these pressures, "the President always gave me the credit of being the most calm and self possessed of any member of the government."

On that morning, however, the navy secretary knew of no immediate steps that could be taken. Flag Officer Louis M. Goldsborough, Commander of the North Atlantic Blockading Squadron, was an able and skillful leader, but he remained down in North Carolina with General Burnside. Equally capable officers on station commanded some of the best and most powerful vessels in the navy, but judging from General Wool's dispatch, they could be of little avail.

Their new ironclad battery should have reached the Roads on Saturday; Welles pinned his reliance upon her. General Wool, however, made no mention of *Monitor* in his last telegram. Welles expected word momentarily from Assistant Secretary Fox or from the senior naval officer on site. But due to another break in the cable, they would not receive Wool's subsequent telegram with news of *Monitor's* arrival until late in the afternoon and would not know of the battle results until evening.

"The most frightened man on that gloomy morning was the Secretary of War," recalled Welles. "He was at times almost frantic. . . ." His words sounded broken and denunciatory. The "panic under which he labored. . .added to the apprehension of others." As recorded in Welles's diary, Stanton did most of the talking. The Rebel ironclad would change the whole character of the war, he exclaimed. She would destroy every naval vessel and take Fort Monroe.

Union soldiers with rifles at attention in front of the unfinished Capitol in May 1861. (loc)

McClellan's campaign against Richmond must be abandoned. Burnside's forces must be recalled or would be captured. The vital blockading base of Port Royal Sound, South Carolina, must be given up. The Confederate ironclad would "come up the Potomac and disperse congress, destroy the Capitol and public buildings, or she might go to New York and Boston and destroy those cities, or levy from them contributions sufficient to carry on the War."

Stanton insisted on warning Northern governors and municipal authorities to take instant measures to protect their harbors. Welles caustically described him peering out the window with an expansive view down the Potomac, expecting a Rebel cannonball to land in the White House before they left the room.

"Foreign intervention would surely follow a succession of events like these, which heated imagination easily called up," observed Nicolay and Hay. "Stanton, unable to control his strong emotion, walked up and down the room like a caged lion. McClellan was dumbfounded and silent. . . . Chase [was] impatient and ready to utter blame; Seward and Welles [were] hopeful, yet without encouraging reasons to justify their hope.

"Lincoln was, as usual in trying moments, composed but eagerly inquisitive, critically scanning the dispatches, interrogating the officers, joining scrap to scrap of information, applying his searching analysis and clear logic to read the danger and find the remedy. . . . The possibilities of the hour were indeed sufficiently portentous to create consternation."

"Most of Stanton's complaints were directed to me," continued the navy secretary, and the others naturally turned to him for information or suggestion. "I had little to impart, except my faith in the untried 'Monitor' experiment, which we had prepared for the emergency."

Stanton inquired about the new vessel, of which he knew little. Welles explained: Had *Monitor* been completed within contract time, they would have sent her up to Norfolk to destroy the Rebel ironclad before she came out of dry dock. When informed that *Monitor* was armed with two guns of large caliber, Stanton returned a "mingled look of incredulity and contempt."

Based on available information, Welles assured them that the converted *Merrimack* was "so cut down and loaded with armor," she could not venture outside of the Capes. She could not pass Kettle Bottom Shoals in the Potomac to "ascend the river and surprise us with a cannon-ball."

Certainly, she could not attack simultaneously every city and harbor on the coast or threaten Burnside's forces in the Carolina Sounds. "It would better become us," he advised, "to calmly consider the situation, and inspire confidence by acting, so far as we could, intelligently, and with discretion and judgment."

Secretary Chase approved this suggestion but thought it might be well to telegraph Governor Morgan and Mayor Opdyke in New York to be on their guard. Welles questioned the propriety of sending abroad panic missives or adding to the general alarm.

A somewhat relieved Secretary Seward turned to Stanton and said they had, perhaps, given way too much to their apprehensions. He saw no alternative except to wait and hear what *Monitor* might accomplish. Welles noted that Seward's sensitive nature could be easily depressed, but he would "promptly rally and catch at hope." Stanton departed abruptly as the morning meeting petered out.

The president ordered his carriage and drove to the Navy Yard to consult with Lieutenant Dahlgren. The esteemed ordnance expert enjoyed the president's regard and confidence, noted Welles, but had not been privy to department plans and could provide no advice, "which seemed to increase the panic." At some point, Lincoln, Stanton, or Seward called General Meigs into the conversation. Welles maintained that Seward had great confidence in Meigs "and deferred to him more than to [Stanton], in all matters of a military character."

This painting depicts the president meeting with his cabinet in July 1862 for the first reading of the Emancipation Proclamation. From left to right: Edwin M. Stanton, Secretary of War, Salmon P. Chase, Secretary of the Treasury, President Lincoln, Gideon Welles, Secretary of the Navy, Caleb B. Smith, Secretary of the Interior, William H. Seward, Secretary of State, Montgomery Blair, Postmaster General, and Edward Bates, Attorney General. (loc)

Naval ordnance expert John A. Dahlgren is pictured here as a rear admiral commanding the South Atlantic Blockading Squadron, ca.1863-1865, next to a 50-pounder Dahlgren rifle. Dahlgren was a friend and confidant of the president, who periodically escaped the White House to confer with him at the Washington Navy Yard. (nhhc)

Dahlgren and Meigs were powerless, Welles opined, "and in full sympathy with Stanton in all his fears and predictions." They were intelligent officers, among the first of their respective professions, "but neither of them was endowed with the fighting qualities of [David G.] Farragut or [William T.] Sherman and in that time of general alarm were not the men to allay panic." Dahlgren did, however, agree with the navy secretary that *Virginia* probably could not ascend the Potomac.

Returning to his house a little before 12:00 p.m., Welles called on Commodore Joseph Smith, to whom he communicated the fate of *Congress*, commanded by his son, Lt. Joseph B. Smith. "The *Congress* sunk!" exclaimed the commodore while buttoning up his coat and looking his friend calmly in the face. "Then Joe is dead."

The secretary suggested that her officers and crew doubtless escaped to the nearby shore. "You don't know Joe as well as I do," said the father. "He would not survive his ship." As Welles noted, "And he did not; but, mortally wounded, perished with her."

Most of the Cabinet met again that sad Sunday afternoon. "A little time and reflection had brought a more calm and resolute feeling," wrote Welles. Except for Stanton, who "spoke out with some fierceness. . .and said he had no expectation of any formidable resistance from any little vessel of two guns against a frigate clothed with iron, nor much confidence in naval officers for such a crisis. If not old fogies, their training was not for this state of things."

The war secretary had telegraphed governors and major cities of the North to take care of themselves, advising that rafts of timber and other obstructions should be placed at the mouths of harbors. John Hay: "The commandants of the harbor defenses at Boston and New York were ordered to stand to their guns, and [Lieutenant] Dahlgren went coolly to work at our Navy Yard here to make the proper preparations to receive the bold rover courteously if she decided to visit the Capital."

Stanton also sent for Cornelius Vanderbilt, the enormously wealthy and influential New York railroad and shipping magnate, to come to Washington for consultation. Vanderbilt, said Stanton to Welles, had large steamers, employed good merchant sailors, and "was a man of resources and great energy."

Vanderbilt's opinion "would be more valuable than that of any other person," meaning the navy secretary or any of his senior officers. Stanton also proposed to block

the Potomac River channel and wished to consult with Dahlgren about it. Welles consented to the consultation but objected to obstructing river navigation.

"The President, though feeling as uncomfortable as any of us, and having his alarm increased by the fears and talk of Stanton, manifested much sympathy and consideration for me," wrote Welles. "My calmness and the suggestions and views I presented were evidently a relief to him, but Stanton's wailings and woeful predictions disturbed him."

Lucius Chittenden called upon his superior, Secretary of the Treasury Chase, after church, but "he had no news, and could give me no comfort." In the afternoon, Chittenden sought information at the war office where the president was usually to be found when any serious fighting was going on. Lincoln was there with a large party including two cabinet members. "It was evident, from the general excitement, that news had been received from the James River."

The chattering telegraph finally disgorged General Wool's lost message of the night before: "The ironclad Ericsson battery *Monitor* has arrived and will proceed to take care of the *Merrimac* in the morning." They awaited the outcome.

Goods and soldiers throng the busy Sixth Street commercial wharf and steamboats in southwest Washington, D.C., ca. 1863. The Mount Vernon Hotel flies the American flag. On the horizon stand the stub of the Washington Monument (left), the Smithsonian Castle, and the U. S. Capitol (with the dome inaccurately portrayed as completed). The White House is behind the Washington Monument. (loc)

With Mutual Fierceness

CHAPTER NINE

MARCH 9, 1862 – EARLY MORNING

The Sabbath dawned bright and clear over Newport News Point, recalled former *Congress* gunner Frederick Curtis. "The warm sun shone over what should have been a quiet scene; but here it did not seem at all like Sunday." Ammunition trains rolled into Camp Butler from Fort Monroe; troops formed up to march out and confront General Magruder. "Everything was bustle, and it was fully expected that there would be a fight that day." He strolled down to the beach where surviving shipmates gathered to watch.

A mile away lay the still-grounded USS *Minnesota* attended by a clutch of steam tugs toward which her sailors flung bags and hammocks, some landing in the water. The little steamer *Dragon* nestled alongside. Men clambered into boats. Barrels of beans, flour, rice, sugar, whiskey—thrown overboard to lighten ship—bobbed on the surface. Guns were being jettisoned. Paymaster William F. Keeler observed from *Monitor* anchored nearby: "Everything seemed in confusion."

"The report every little while through the night that the *Merrimac* was coming kept all [*Monitor*] hands to quarters," Keeler wrote to his wife. "No one slept." Mist lifting from the water revealed the CSS *Virginia* with her consorts two miles across the Roads under Confederate batteries at Sewell's Point with steam rising from their stacks and bows swinging toward *Minnesota*. The Rebels began their day, according to one of *Virginia's* marines, "with two jiggers of whiskey and a hearty breakfast."

Monitor's commanding officer, Lt. John L. Worden, inquired of *Minnesota's* Captain Gershom J. Van Brunt

John Ericsson designed this unique, four-fluked anchor to fit the round anchor well in *Monitor's* bow. Constructed of wrought iron, the anchor weighs over one thousand pounds. It was recovered from the wreck site in 1983 and is on display at the *Monitor Center*. (mmp)

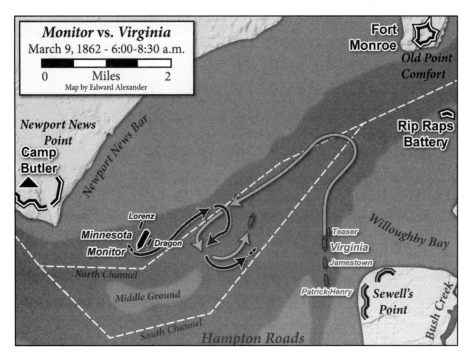

Monitor vs. Virginia
March 9, 1862 - 6:00-8:30 a.m.

0   Miles   2
Map by Edward Alexander

Fort Monroe
Old Point Comfort

Newport News Point
Camp Butler

Newport News Bar

Rip Raps Battery

Lorenz

Minnesota
Dragon
Monitor

Willoughby Bay

Teaser
Virginia
Jamestown

North Channel

Middle Ground

Patrick Henry

Sewell's Point

Bush Creek

South Channel

Hampton Roads

Monitor vs. Virginia 1— As Virginia approaches Minnesota, Monitor appears from behind the big frigate. The ironclads exchange their first volleys and begin circling.

what he should do. "If I cannot lighten my ship off [the shoal] I shall destroy her," Van Brunt declared. "I will stand by you to the last if I can help you," said Worden. "No sir, you cannot help me," came the reply.

Worden descended to *Monitor's* crowded berth deck where exhausted crewmen huddled in the dim light of oil lanterns over breakfast of hardtack, canned roast beef, and coffee. They all had volunteered, he reminded them. But having seen what *Virginia* was capable of and considering the fate of *Cumberland*, did any regret joining? If so, they would be sent aboard *Roanoke*.

The crew leaped to their feet and gave three cheers. Not one took the offer as breakfast and coffee were forgotten. At 7:20 a.m., Worden piped all hands to quarters and got underway. "Our fastenings were cast off, our machinery started, and we moved out to meet [*Virginia*] half-way. We had come a long way to fight her, and did not intend to lose our opportunity."

"[*Minnesota's*] wooden sides shewed terrible traces of the conflict," continued Keeler, where enemy rounds had struck the day before. "The idea of assistance or protection being offered to the huge thing by the little pigmy at her side seemed absolutely ridiculous." Judging by "curt & crispy" shouts raining down from *Minnesota's* high decks, her sailors thought so too. "As the *Merrimac* approached, we slowly steamed out of the shadow of our towering friend no ways daunted by her rather ungracious replies."

Others shared the skepticism. Frederick Curtis with his *Cumberland* shipmates at Newport News: "To tell the truth, we did not have much faith in the 'Monitor'; We all expected to see the 'Merrimac' destroy her." He watched from the top of a tree. Fireman Joseph McDonald on *Dragon*: "There was the little *Monitor* flat on the water like a turtle. We all commenced to comment on her and make fun. 'Pshaw! That thing? Why, we could lick her ourselves!'" After all, *Monitor* had two guns to *Virginia's* ten.

The Rebel ironclad turned up North Channel heading directly for *Minnesota's* vulnerable stern. Anticipating this move during the night, Captain Van Brunt had hauled two 9-inch broadside guns to the aft ports in his cabin. *Virginia* opened with her bow gun. "Her first shot struck the water and bounded toward us, but fell short," recalled McDonald.

Paymaster Keeler and Surgeon Daniel C. Logue stood out on *Monitor's* open deck with Captain Worden, watching the still distant enemy. A puff of smoke arose from her; a shell howled over their heads, burst a large hole through *Minnesota's* ensign, and crashed into the main deck.

The next shot plunged into the frigate's stern at the water line near the magazine but fortunately did not penetrate. *Virginia* closed to about a mile while *Minnesota* responded with her aft guns. Worden ordered the two officers below, following them up the turret side ladder and down the sliding hatch on top, which banged shut behind them.

Within this dim, claustrophobic, metal drum—20 feet in diameter—behind eight inches of iron squatted the two immense 11-inch, muzzle-loading Dahlgren guns. Dim daylight filtered down through ventilation holes in the iron plates overhead reflecting off whitewashed walls. Removable floor grates alongside the guns provided access below when aligned with a corresponding hatch in the main deck.

Executive Officer Lt. Samuel D. Greene supervised the weapons assisted by Acting Master Louis N. Stodder and Chief Engineer Alban C. Stimers. Sixteen brawny sailors, packed in eight to a gun, would load and ram home shot on top of powder cartridges, then haul the massive weapons forward to firing positions. When the gun fired and recoiled into the turret, they cleared the bores with long-handled worms and sponges, then reloaded. Boatswain's Mate John Stocking and Seaman Thomas Lochrane served as gun captains.

None of these men had been drilled on these guns or in this turret. As Worden, Keeler, and Logue passed through to the berth deck below, one crew hoisted a 165-pound shot into the maw of their Dahlgren. "Send them that with my complements, my lads," instructed the captain.

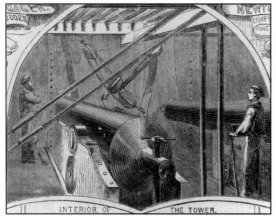

This—inaccurately scaled—*Harper's Weekly* engraving (1862) depicts *Monitor's* turret interior. Note heavy blocks and tackle for lifting the port pendulums. The sailor at right is manning the lever controlling steam to the turret drive engines, with which he starts, stops, and reverses turret motion. (nhhc)

Worden took station on the pilothouse platform 50 feet forward near the bow, his head and shoulders in the box. A small gap, less than an inch, between the iron beams provided a low and narrow but all-around view. Jammed at his elbow was Acting Master Samuel Howard, the volunteer pilot. Quartermaster Peter Williams grabbed the helm and steered throughout the engagement.

On the berth deck behind them, Acting Master John N. Webber had charge of the powder division aided by Gunner's Mate Joseph Crown. They stood below the turret, ready to pass up powder and shell. To the rear in the engine and fire rooms, First Assistant Engineer Isaac Newton and his team oversaw the machinery.

"A few straggling rays of light found their way from the top of the tower to the depths below," wrote Keeler. "Every one was at his post, fixed like a statue, the most profound silence reigned—if there had been a coward heart there, its throb would have been audible, so *intense* was the stillness. I experienced a peculiar sensation, I do not think it was fear, but it was different from anything I ever knew before.

"We were enclosed in what we supposed to be an impenetrable armour—we knew that a powerful foe was about to meet us—ours was an untried experiment & our enemy's first fire might make it a coffin for us all. . . . The suspense was awful as we waited in the dim light expecting every moment to hear the crash of our enemy's shot."

Crewman David Ellis: "Everything seemed so still, so peaceable, so serene, as if soothed and tranquilized and beautiful by a special benediction from heaven." None of these anxious men—except three in the pilot house—could see out or could know when or from what direction the attack would come.

"Now mark the condition our men and officers were in," wrote Lieutenant Greene to his parents after the fight. *Monitor* had barely escaped shipwreck twice within the past 36 hours and for 48 hours, few if any slept or ate anything but hard bread. They labored all night. "As for myself, I had not slept a wink for 51 hours, and had been on my feet almost constantly. But after the first gun was fired, we forgot all fatigues, hard work and everything else, and went to work fighting as hard as men ever fought."

To the astonishment of Captain Van Brunt, Worden charged directly for *Virginia*, placing his little vessel between *Minnesota* and the foe: "The contrast was that of a pigmy to a giant," he noted. *Virginia's* little wooden consorts turned and headed back the way they had come.

In the gloom below, Keeler heard the muffled whump of a gun, then another and another, then a thunderous broadside. "The infernal howl (I can't give it a more appropriate name) of the shells as they flew over our vessel was all that broke the silence & made it seem still more terrible." Still at long range and employing the common tactic of ricochet—aiming guns low, skipping shots along the surface—*Virginia* and *Minnesota* blasted away, occasionally hitting *Monitor*. Rounds could make 20 to 40 skips.

Monitor was equipped with a speaking tube—a brass pipe through which voice orders and status reports could be exchanged between pilothouse and turret—but it did not work. "The situation was novel," noted Greene. While engaged in desperate combat, the captain—commanding and guiding the warship— found himself enclosed in one place while the executive officer—directing the weapons—was shut in another. Communication proved "difficult and uncertain."

Paymaster Keeler and Captain's Clerk Daniel Toffey were assigned as runners passing verbal messages between stations, a 150-foot round trip amidst the clamor of engines and thunder of guns and shells. "They performed their work with zeal and alacrity," Greene reported, "but, both being landsmen, our technical communications sometimes miscarried."

Lieutenant Greene's best—and most dangerous— view for aiming was through the few-inch gap between the gun muzzle and the top of the gun port, but only with the gun run out for firing. With the guns in, port covers were closed for protection. Greene called down the hatch in the turret floor to Keeler below, instructing him to go forward and ask the captain for permission to fire. The

One of the most accurate and dramatic renderings of the engagement is this painting by Julian O. Davidson (1853-1894), "Monitor and Merrimac: First Fight Between Ironclads" (1885). Davidson was one of America's most renowned marine painters, producing numerous well-known works on War of 1812 and Civil War naval battles, which were widely distributed as lithographs and prints. (loc)

Gershom Jacques Van Brunt, Captain USN (1798-1863) had 42 years' service. Concerning *Monitor's* timely arrival in Hampton Roads, he wrote: "All on board felt we had a friend that would stand by us in our hour of trial." (nhhc)

reply: "Tell Mr. Greene not to fire till I give the word, to be cool & deliberate, to take sure aim & not to waste a shot."

Captain Worden: "At this time. . .I was approaching [*Virginia*] on her starboard bow, on a course nearly at right angles with her line of keel, reserving my fire until near enough that every shot might take effect." He closed to about a third of a mile, altered course, stopped the engine, and ordered, "Commence firing!"

Hauled by the gunners, the mammoth port cover rumbled open; the gun grumbled forward on its rollers; the big black muzzle protruded; the recoil friction brake was engaged. Greene snatched a look over the barrel top, took aim, stepped back, and yanked the firelock string at 8:20 a.m.

The entire structure throbbed and trembeled with a deafening concussion as the behemoth lept inward. "And thus commenced the great battle between the '*Monitor*' and '*Merrimac*'. . . . Every shot I would ask the Captain the effect, and the majority of them were encouraging."

"O, what a relief it was," wrote Keeler. "The gun over my head thundered out its challenge with a report which jarred our vessel, but it was music to us all." *Virginia* apparently took no notice of the strange craft until a second shot made "her iron scales rattle." The Rebel ironclad turned her head upstream against the tide until nearly stationary and replied with a starboard broadside of grape and canister followed by musketry, "which rattled on our iron deck like hailstones" but caused no damage.

A *Monitor* gunner stuck his head out the port for a look. "The d...d fools are firing canister at us," he exclaimed with a grin. These rounds—loaded for action against the wooden *Minnesota* and her men—had no effect on them. *Virginia* immediately switched to solid shot and shell.

Primary structural elements of the turret and guns with customized carriages. The hand wheel on the gun carriage tightened or loosened friction pads between the gun slide rails, dampening recoil. The fore-aft diagonal braces are not on *Monitor* plans or subsequent depictions. They evidently were added during construction to stabilize the turret and were unknown until revealed by the turret's recovery. The perforated tower deck plates were similarly discovered. *Graphic by J. M. Caiella.* (jmc)

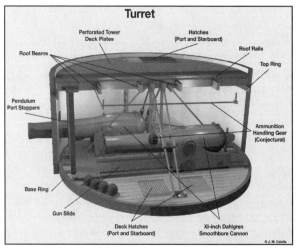

Turret

Perforated Tower Deck Plates
Hatches (Port and Starboard)
Roof Rails
Roof Beams
Top Ring
Pendulum Port Stoppers
Ammunition Handling Gear (Conjectural)
Base Ring
Gun Slide
Deck Hatches (Port and Starboard)
XI-inch Dahlgren Smoothbore Cannon
© J. M. Caiella

When the first of these clanged against the turret, the gunners cringed in consternation, reported Engineer Stimers to his father. The engineer locked eyes with them and asked, "Did the shot come through?" "No sir," one replied, "but it made a big dent, just look there sir!" "A big dent," Stimers retorted, "of course it made a big dent—that is just what we expected, but what do you care as long as it keeps out the shot?" "Oh! It's all right then of course sir."

Stimers thought the turret was "a splendid structure," but for Captain Worden it had worrisome weaknesses. The 120-ton drum hung from its central, vertical spindle supported by iron braces. The base of the shaft rested below on a wedge-shaped key, which could be inserted or withdrawn by turning a large bolt with a wrench.

When not in combat, the key was disengaged, lowering and resting the turret circumference on a brass ring in the deck; it could not rotate. Inserting the key for combat raised the turret, floating it 2¾ inches above the deck and allowing it to turn.

Worden expected that a projectile striking the curved exterior at an acute angle would glance off harmlessly. But if fired squarely in line with the vertical axis, the turret would take the whole force of the blow; the entire structure could be deformed, jamming the revolving mechanism. "Then we would be wholly disabled."

The captain also feared that hundreds of bolt and rivet heads holding together 192 1-inch iron plates in eight layers would blast off inside when hit outside, creating lethal projectiles amongst the men. Ericsson had installed another layer of thin iron plating or "mantelets" covering the interior to mitigate this risk.

Worden afterward described the effect of a 150-pound projectile hitting straight on from 30 yards. Without cracking or splitting the iron, it created a smooth dent, "a perfect mold" of the shell, 2.5 inches deep, which bulged right through 8 inches of armor. "If anything could test the turret, it was that shot. . . . It did not start a rivet-head or a nut! I touched the lever—the turret revolved as smoothly as before. The turret had stood the test; I could mark that point of weakness off my list forever."

Worden had another worry going in: *Monitor's* armored deck joined the hull at a right angle—what sailors call the "plank shear"—which he believed to be her weakest point.

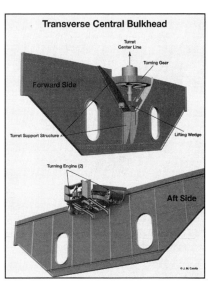

Monitor's transverse bulkhead is the only structural bulkhead in the hull. It supports the turret shaft, drive gear, and drive engines. *Graphic by J. M. Caiella.* (jmc)

A shell striking just there would concentrate its energy. "It might open a seam in the hull below the water-line, or pierce the wooden hull, and sink us. . . ." At the second exchange, with *Virginia* returning six or eight rounds to *Monitor's* two, another of her shells struck the plank shear at its angle tearing up one of the deck-plates.

Despite enemy sharpshooters, the captain felt compelled to investigate. He ordered one of the port shutters hauled aside, slid out, walked to the side, and lay down upon his chest to peer over the edge. "The hull was uninjured, except for a few splinters in the wood. I walked back and crawled into the turret— the bullets were falling on the iron deck all about me as thick as hail-stones in a storm." With the vessel moving and turning, he made a small target lying down.

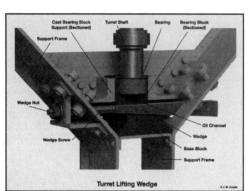

Turret Lifting Wedge

To raise the turret and allow it to rotate, engineers turned the wedge nut with a large wrench, drawing the wedge inward and pushing the shaft up until the bottom of the turret's circumference floated above the deck by 2 ¾". In this position the entire weight of the structure rested through the shaft on the bearing block, wedge, and base block. The shaft turned in the oiled bearing block. Backing the nut lowered the turret onto the deck, locking it in place. It is not surprising that Captain Worden was concerned about the stability of this mechanism when struck by enemy fire. This design was not optimal and would not be continued in subsequent monitors. *Graphic by J. M. Caiella.* (jmc)

"The *Merrimac* could not sink us if we let her pound us for a month," announced Worden. "The men cheered; the knowledge put new life into all." Lieutenant Greene: "A look of confidence passed over the men's faces and we believed the *Merrimac* would not repeat the work she had accomplished the day before."

As both vessels came within the arc of *Minnesota's* main battery broadsides, *Monitor* was hit at least twice from friendly fire. One of the engineers reported to his wife: "It don't make much difference who fires at us."

"Ironclad against ironclad," recalled Engineer Stimers. "We maneuvered about the bay here and went at each other with mutual fierceness." They circled awkwardly in what would appear to a modern observer as slow motion. Guns bellowed as fast as they could be served. Choking white smoke shot with flame erupted from their maws.

Rounds screamed, clanged, boomed, and splashed all around. Engines thumped and clanked; blowers roared. Black clouds billowed from stacks. Big propellers thrashed the water. Men trapped inside, many stripped to the waist with scraps of cloth around their ears, shouted, sweated, and struggled to manage their metal monsters. The gunners were "covered with powder & smoke, the perspiration falling from them like rain," noted Keeler.

"We. . .were often within a ship's length [of *Monitor*]," reported *Virginia* executive officer and now acting captain, Lt. Catesby ap R. Jones. "Once while passing we fired a broadside at her only a few yards distant. She and her turret appeared to be under perfect control. Her light draft enabled her to move about us at pleasure." He tried unsuccessfully to draw *Monitor* within range of Confederate batteries on Sewell's Point.

"Five times during the engagement we touched each other," wrote Lieutenant Greene, "and each time I

fired a gun at [*Virginia*], and I will vouch the 168 lbs. penetrated her sides. . . . The shot, shell, grape, canister, musket and rifle balls flew about us in every direction, but did us no damage. Our Tower was struck several times, and though the noise was pretty loud, it did not effect us any."

Acting Master Stodder incautiously leaned against the turret bulkhead just as a Rebel shot whanged against the outside flinging him clean over the guns to the deck, knocking him senseless, and injuring his knee. Seaman Peter Trescott's head was only inches from the point of impact. "I dropped like a dead man," he recalled.

Both were carried below where Surgeon Logue administered stimulants and applied cold presses. They recovered fully by the following morning, the only battle casualties among the crew. Engineer Stimers also was flung down, but had only his hand against the bulkhead. "I immediately jumped up again and did not leave my duties."

Massive, coffin-shaped wrought-iron pendulums covered the ports while the Dahlgrens were being loaded. A loophole in each shutter allowed gunners to awkwardly thrust out their long tool handles to sponge and worm residue from hot barrels after each shot, and to ram home fresh rounds.

The entire gun crew hauled on a block and tackle to move one of these heavy port lids and, because they swung inward toward each other, only one could be opened while the other remained closed (a design flaw that would be corrected in later monitors). Only one gun could be fired at a time, a cumbersome and slow process.

"The effect upon one shut up in a revolving drum is perplexing," wrote Greene, "and it is not a simple matter to keep the bearings." In addition to the narrow opening above the barrel, the lieutenant could peer out through small sight holes to the left and right or directly behind the guns.

This photo of the sub-turret chamber in the monitor USS *Catskill* displays typically constrained machinery spaces. The turret central shaft rests on its bearing and base blocks. Note that the lifting mechanism now uses a rack and pinion device in place of the *Monitor's* wedge. *Catskill* was commissioned in December 1863 as a *Passaic*-class monitor, the next class after the original. (nhhc)

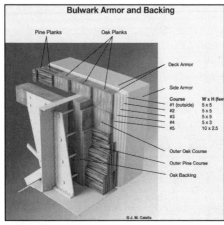

Bulwark Armor and Backing

Pine Planks   Oak Planks

Deck Armor

Side Armor

Course	W x H (feet)
#1 (outside)	5 x 5
#2	5 x 5
#3	5 x 5
#4	5 x 3
#5	10 x 2.5

Outer Oak Course

Outer Pine Course

Oak Backing

© J. M. Caiella

This cross section of *Monitor's* armor shows layers of iron and wood on the deck and overhang. The deck armor was two layers of ½-inch wrought iron, courses laid transversely over oak and pine planks. The side armor was 5 layers of 1-inch plates of decreasing height over oak and pine backing. Captain Worden worried about enemy shells striking the vulnerable corner where side armor met deck armor. *Graphic by J. M. Caiella.* (jmc)

These nearly useless view ports made favorite targets for eager muskets on *Virginia*. White reference marks had been chalked on the main deck below the turret floor grating to indicate port and starboard, bow and stern, but these marks were obliterated early on probably by soot from the guns and sweat from the gunners.

Both vessels moved continuously—turning, backing, and forwarding—while the turret spun independently. A mostly blind and frequently disoriented lieutenant had difficulty not only knowing where the enemy was, but also how the gun muzzles pointed relative to his own vessel.

Greene passed a stream of "How does the *Merrimac* bear?" questions to the pilothouse via the runners. With unavoidable delay and continuous change, Worden replied: "On the starboard beam" or "On the port-quarter," as might be. But in what direction was the starboard beam or the port quarter or any other bearing? He had no useful points of reference.

The lieutenant worried, first, to prevent enemy projectiles from entering through an open gun port; a shell exploding inside would end the fight and there were no relief gun crews. And second: "A careless or impatient hand, during the confusion arising from the whirligig motion of the tower," might fire into the pilothouse directly in front. "For this and other reasons, I fired every gun while I remained in the turret."

To make matters worse, the working of the turret was "not altogether satisfactory." Auxiliary steam engines below the deck drove rotation through large horizontal gears connected to the central shaft.

One man operated a crank handle between the guns, admitting or throttling steam to the drive engines to start, stop, or reverse the turret. Like all *Monitor's* machinery, these mechanisms were undergoing their first combat trial. The operation was imprecise, with gears probably rusted from the wet trip down the coast.

A brief test run in New York six days earlier established that the turret turned at two and a half

Turret Roof and Stopper Detail

Perforated Splinter Plates

Rails

Stopper Thimble

Stopper Rail

Guide Pieces and Rivets

Stopper

Stopper Port
1" diameter exterior
6" diameter interior

© J. M. Caiella

Monitor turret roof and gunport stopper detail. *Graphic by J. M. Caiella.* (jmc)

revolutions per minute under 25 pounds of steam. But during the engagement, even Engineer Stimers—who was "an active, muscular man," according to Greene—found the turret unmanageable. It was very slow to start and once moving, slow to stop, even slower to reverse. "The conditions were very different from those of an ordinary broadside gun, under which we had been trained on wooden ships."

Finding it nearly impossible to stop rotation in line of fire, open the heavy gun port cover, and sight and shoot at a target that was itself moving, Greene settled on a pattern: Rotate the turret away from *Virginia* and stop to load leaving gun ports open to save time and effort. Then when ready, start revolving again and fire "on the fly" as the target swept past the muzzles. He could fire both guns at a faster rate.

This view looks forward on the starboard side of *Monitor's* deck, July 9, 1862. Note the iron plating on deck and turret, and Rebel shell dents. A steel cable wraps the top of the turret. The sloping sides of the boxy pilothouse (just forward and to right of the turret) were added after the battle to deflect enemy rounds. The officers are (left to right): Third Assistant Engineer Robinson W. Hands, Acting Master Louis N. Stodder, Second Assistant Engineer Albert B. Campbell (seated) and Acting Volunteer Lieutenant William Flye (with binoculars). (nhhc)

Soldiers and civilians mobbed both shorelines that morning. A Georgia infantryman named Sam McKee could not get a pass but went anyway. The bridge guard would not let him through without the pass. "I give a niger a half a dollar to carry me across [the stream] in a bateau and then I had to walk some six miles" where he found the beach "covered for miles up and down the bay [with people] witnessing the great fighting."

"The *Virginia* is discouragingly cumbrous and unwieldly," recalled Confederate Army Capt. William Norris. Her turning radius was ³⁄₄ mile. Fifteen minutes of maneuvering were required between broadsides just to repoint the guns, and then they had no more effect, "than if we had thrown marbles at her." Meanwhile, "The *Monitor* is whirling around and about like a top. . . . Her precise and rapid movement elicits the wonder and admiration of all."

Another Southerner, Sallie Brock Putnam, observed that *Monitor* was "of midnight hue, which, like a thing of darkness, moved about with spirit-like rapidity."

Nearly Every Shot Struck

CHAPTER TEN
MARCH 9, 1862 – MID MORNING TO EARLY AFTERNOON

Virginia's Lt. John Taylor Wood had been expecting *Monitor*, but "she could not possibly have made her appearance at a more inopportune time," interrupting their determination to destroy *Minnesota* and the fleet around Fort Monroe. "She appeared but a pigmy compared with the lofty frigate which she guarded. But in her size was one great element of her success. . . . The *Monitor* was firing every seven or eight minutes, and nearly every shot struck."

"When her turret revolved we could see nothing but two immense guns," recalled a Rebel marine. Those guns bellowed and promptly disappeared while his gun crew scrambled to respond. Acting Captain Catesby ap R. Jones wondered how the Yankees could take aim so quickly: "The *Virginia*, however, was a large target and generally so near that the *Monitor's* shot did not often miss. It did not appear to us that our shell had any effect upon the *Monitor*. We had no solid shot."

Virginia had been loaded with explosive shells to penetrate and demolish the U.S. Navy's wooden walls, but against iron, shells detonated on the surface and dissipated their energy externally. Solid shot had more concentrated smashing power, but only a few rounds had been supplied for the hot-shot guns (which had destroyed *Congress*), and they were quickly expended.

Lieutenant John M. Brooke had been testing armor-piercing steel bolts for his Brooke rifles using a test target based on Northern newspaper drawings of *Monitor's* turret, but the bolts were not yet available. Confederates would claim that solid shot and/or bolts would have

This copper commemorative coin, dated 1863, was the size of a modern penny but yellower in color. (mmp)

This popular but inaccurate Currier and Ives illustration (ca. 1862) is titled: "Terrific combat between the 'Monitor' 2 guns & 'Merrimac' 10 guns. The first fight between iron clad ships of war, in Hampton Roads, March 9th 1862, in which the little 'Monitor' whipped the 'Merrimac' and the whole 'school' of Rebel steamers." Note among other errors the pointed peak of *Virginia's* casemate. (loc)

disabled or destroyed the Union ironclad, one of several contentious "what ifs" of the engagement.

The men on *Virginia's* more traditional gun deck had a full day of hot combat under their belts. Unlike their opponents, they knew their weapons and their ship—still solid after a severe battering. "The only damage [*Monitor*] did was to the armor," reported Jones. Most hits were oblique, caroming off the inclined surface, cracking the iron plates and sometimes blowing away large chunks of the external layer, but not damaging the two feet of oak and pine backing.

A few missiles connecting at right angles cracked but did not penetrate the backing. In several instances, two or more adjacent blows displaced additional iron and bulged the wood inside. "Generally the shot were much scattered. . . . The shield was never pierced though it was evident that two shots striking in the same place would have made a large hole through everything."

Monitor's Engineer Stimers found fault with the only ammunition fired from their Dahlgrens during the fight: 11-inch solid cast-iron round shot. The difficulty was not lack of penetration but "want of homogeneity" (irregularities in roundness or "windage") causing them "to go almost anywhere except where the gun was aimed."

Another "what if" controversy concerns the Navy Department orders for Worden to use only 15-pound half charges. Had *Monitor's* guns been loaded with full charges (which afterward did test safely and were used), Lieutenant Greene later argued, their rounds would have penetrated *Virginia's* armor.

"Not a single shot struck [*Virginia*] at the water-line," added Confederate Lieutenant Wood, "where the ship was utterly unprotected and where one would have been fatal. Or had the fire been concentrated on any one spot, the shield would have been pierced; or had larger charges been used, the result would have been the same."

One of *Virginia's* sailors, Richard Curtis, and shipmate Benjamin Sheriff were ordered to grab rifles and "shoot the first man that you see" on *Monitor* by aiming at open gun and viewing ports in the pilothouse and turret. The two men took station behind gun ports on either side of the forward pivot gun, which pointed directly ahead through its centerline port leaving the angled bow ports unoccupied.

Curtis was to starboard and Sheriff to port, "both on our knees, but not in prayer." Curtis readied his weapon and peered cautiously out at *Monitor* looming alongside. Sheriff frantically called out, "look out Curtis, look out Curtis" just as the maw of a big Dahlgren rotated into view staring them squarely in the face. "Sheriff and myself thought it was time to move, which we did quickly. Saw no man, fired no gun."

While *Virginia's* gundeck was all "bustle, smoke, grimy figures, and stern commands," recalled Assistant Engineer H. Ashton Ramsay, "down in the engine and boiler rooms the sixteen furnaces were belching out fire and smoke." Firemen toiled before the flames "like so many gladiators" shoveling and stirring coal, intensifying combustion and heat.

"The noise of the cracking, roaring fires, escaping steam, and the loud and labored pulsations of the engines, together with the roar of battle above and the thud and vibration of the huge masses of iron which were hurled against us produced a scene and sound to be compared only with the poet's picture of the lower regions."

Lieutenant Wood said, "More than two hours had passed, and we had made no impression on the enemy so far as we could discover, while our wounds were slight. Several times the *Monitor* ceased firing, and we were in hopes she was disabled, but the revolution again of her turret and the heavy blows of her 11-inch shot on our sides soon undeceived us."

Across the way in *Monitor's* turret, the supply of shot ran out. Captain John Worden hauled off out of action to replenish from the magazine below. Powder cartridges weighing 15 pounds could be lifted easily from the lower deck, but hauling up 165-pound shot by block and tackle was slow and tedious. The turret remained stationary to align the floor grating next to each gun with the hatch in the main deck. Worden again climbed out the gun port onto the open deck to view his vessel's condition before renewing the fight.

Acting Captain Jones seized the opportunity for *Virginia* to bear down upon *Minnesota*. Captain Van Brunt opened up with his port battery and 10-inch pivot, "a

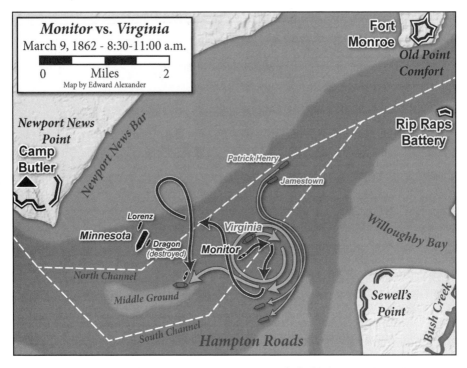

Monitor vs. Virginia 2— Monitor hauls off to replenish ammunition supply; *Virginia* bombards *Minnesota* and destroys *Dragon* but runs aground; *Monitor* charges back in.

broadside," he reported, "which would have blown out of water any timber-built ship in the world."

A shell from *Virginia's* bow gun crashed through the frigate's hull, blowing four rooms into one, exploding powder charges, starting a fire, and, wrote Midshipman Cotton, "demoralizing the after powder division generally, the bandsmen in particular, and creating havoc and panic among their instruments." Crewmen promptly extinguished the fire.

The little steam tug *Dragon* still lay alongside *Minnesota* with the frigate's guns roaring over and around her. The tug's sailors—among them Fireman Joseph McDonald—kept their heads down. But *Dragon* obstructed the lower tier guns and was ordered to move away. McDonald sprang forward to cast off a mooring line. "Just then I met my fate," he recalled.

A *Virginia* shell exploded on *Dragon's* boiler amidships, flinging McDonald down, ripping his left leg with shrapnel and splitting the thigh bone. "The air was so full of burning powder, steam, and smoke that in my half-stunned condition I thought I was suffocating in the water, and struck out as if to swim; but strong hands pulled me through a port-hole of the *Minnesota* and laid me out on the deck.

"The roar of the battle continued, but my fighting was over. The long and the short of it is, that one of my burial-places is in Old Virginia, as I told a friend, there is where I left my leg. Other poor fellows on the *Dragon* were frightfully scalded."

Like fellow Union captains, Van Brunt recruited contraband and freedmen to fill out a chronically undermanned crew, treating them as he would any enlistments. The powerful aft pivot gun was manned solely by African-Americans. "Negroes fought energetically and bravely—none more so," he reported. "They evidently felt that they were thus working at the deliverance of their race." Two "coloreds" were wounded: Joyce Moore and Eli Parris.

Van Brunt concentrated "an incessant fire" from *Minnesota's* gun deck, upper deck, and forecastle pivot gun. "At least fifty solid shot struck [*Virginia*] on her slanting side without producing any apparent effect." But as *Virginia* turned away to escape this bombardment, wrote Engineer Ramsay, "an accident occurred that threatened our utter destruction. We stuck fast aground on a sand-bar. Our situation was critical." *Patrick Henry* and *Jamestown* tried to assist at great risk to themselves.

This artwork published in *Deeds of Valor,* 1907, is titled "The Monitor's Heros at work in the Turret." (nhhc)

Then *Monitor* came charging back, right up to the immovable and slightly heeled over Rebel ironclad, steaming circles around her, picking bow and stern angles where few opposing guns could be pointed, and blasting away at every chink in her armor. Every chink, "but that which was actually vulnerable, had she known it."

Virginia had lost her heavy iron ram the day before along with an anchor, while two days' fighting and maneuvering had consumed much coal. She sat higher in the water, uncovering a strip of wooden hull below the shield. "These exposed portions rendered us no longer an ironclad," Ramsay noted, "and the *Monitor* might have pierced us between wind and water had she depressed her guns." It was *Virginia's* "heel of Achilles." They had to get her off that sandbank.

Ramsay continued: "We lashed down the safety valves, heaped quick-burning combustibles into the already raging fires, and brought the boilers to a pressure that would have been unsafe under ordinary

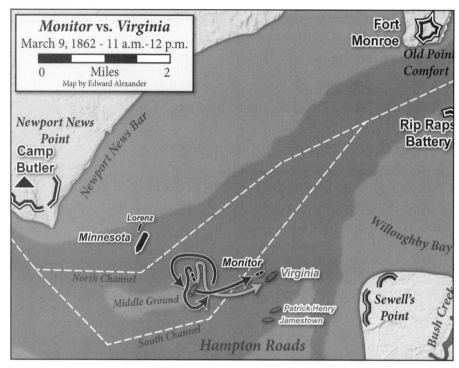

Monitor vs. Virginia
March 9, 1862 - 11 a.m.-12 p.m.

0   Miles   2
Map by Edward Alexander

Fort Monroe

Old Point Comfort

Newport News Point

Camp Butler

Newport News Bar

Rip Raps Battery

Lorenz

Minnesota

Monitor

Virginia

Willoughby Bay

North Channel

Middle Ground

Patrick Henry

Jamestown

Sewell's Point

Bush Creek

South Channel

Hampton Roads

Monitor vs. Virginia 3— Afloat again, Virginia steams down the bay with Monitor in pursuit.

circumstances. The propeller churned the mud and water furiously, but the ship did not stir. We piled on oiled cotton waste, splints of wood, anything that would burn faster than coal."

"It seemed impossible that the boilers could stand the pressure we were crowding upon them. Just as we were beginning to despair there was a perceptible movement, and the *Merrimac* slowly dragged herself off the shoal by main strength. We were saved."

Virginia shot back at *Minnesota* whenever her weapons would bear. "We set [*Minnesota*] on fire and did her serious injury, though much less than we then supposed," wrote Lieutenant Jones. "Generally the distance was too great for effective firing." He had intended to close within half a mile and complete her destruction, but never came closer than a mile.

Confederate Army Capt. William Norris watched from Sewell's Point: "We have knocked a hole into [*Minnesota*], large enough to admit a wagon and four horses, driving four of her ports into one, and the carnage in and about her had been dreadful. Of the officers and crew of a steamer alongside, not one remained alive I believe."

Afloat and moving again, *Virginia* charged down the bay with *Monitor* in pursuit. Jones attempted to lure

Monitor into a position to ram and board her. Lieutenant Wood: "For nearly an hour we manoeuvred for a position. Now 'Go ahead!' now 'Stop!' now 'Astern!' The ship was as unwieldy as Noah's ark. At last an opportunity offered. 'Go ahead, full speed!'"

But before the lumbering ironclad gathered headway, Worden put *Monitor's* helm hard a port, opening the angle between the two vessels and avoiding direct impact. *Virginia* glanced off without inflicting damage. Chief Engineer Ramsay: "I did not feel the slightest shock down in the engine-room, though we struck her fairly enough." The engineer thought Jones was overly concerned about crushing the bow, now unprotected by the ram, and reversed engines prematurely.

Worden on *Monitor* noted: "It gave us a shock, pushed us around, and that was all the harm. But the movement placed our sides together. I gave her two guns, which I think lodged in her side, for, from my lookout crack, I could not see that either shot rebounded. Ours being the smaller vessel, and more easily handled, I had no difficulty in avoiding her ram." Back aft in *Monitor's* engine room, Engineer Stimers called it "a tremendous thump" but harmless. "She will not try that again." After the battle, he could hardly identify the point of contact.

The collision caused *Monitor's* sharp upper deck edge to cut deep into *Virginia's* broad wooden stem, twisting it and starting an alarming but temporary leak. Jones called twice for information from Engineer Ramsay, who assured him there was no water in the engine and boiler rooms. "With the two large Worthington pumps, besides the bilge injections, we could keep her afloat for hours, even with a ten-inch shell in her hull."

Had *Virginia's* ram remained in place, Confederates later claimed, *Monitor* would have gone down like *Cumberland*. Worden disagreed: *Virginia* could not have damaged *Monitor* "a particle more by the blow" particularly at such short range and slow speed. The ram would have struck the deck edge where iron and wood backing were thickest, and the ram was not long enough to impact *Monitor's* thin lower hull.

As *Monitor* slipped by, Lieutenant Greene planted another shot "fair and square" upon the forward

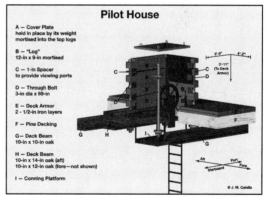

Pilot House

A — Cover Plate held in place by its weight mortised into the top logs

B — "Log" 12-in x 9-in mortised

C — 1-in Spacer to provide viewing ports

D — Through Bolt 3-in dia x 69-in

E — Deck Armor 2 - 1/2-in iron layers

F — Pine Decking

G — Deck Beam 10-in x 10-in oak

H — Deck Beam 10-in x 14-in oak (aft) 10-in x 12-in oak (fore—not shown)

I — Conning Platform

© J. M. Caiella

A schematic of *Monitor's* pilothouse constructed of iron logs. It was a constrained space for three men. When criticized about the pilothouse after the battle, John Ericsson countered that he had intended to place it on top of the turret (as was done on later monitors) but did not have time for the complex design and engineering. *Graphic by J. M. Caiella.* (jmc) casemate, but "the shot rebounded without doing any more damage than possibly to start some of the beams of her armor-backing." *Monitor* ran around the Rebel ironclad again, intentionally battering at spots hit before. Worden: "Those shots must have been effective, for they were followed by a shower of bars of iron."

"Our ship [*Virginia*] was working worse and worse," reported Lieutenant Wood. Loss of the smokestack impeded exhaust of the boiler fires. Fumes choked engineering spaces and gundeck; steam pressure went down along with the vessel's momentum. Once or twice the ship was on the bottom. They were confined to a narrow channel, while the shallower-draft *Monitor* could take any position, "and always have us in range of her guns."

Descending from the deck atop *Virginia's* casemate, Acting Captain Jones observed a gun division standing at ease and inquired of the officer in charge why he was not firing. "Why, our powder is very precious," replied Lieutenant Eggleston. "I find that I can do her about as much damage by snapping my thumb at her every two minutes and a half."

Lieutenant Wood: "Again [*Monitor*] came up on our quarter, her bow against our side, and at this distance fired twice." Both shots struck halfway up the shield near the aft pivot gun, humping the entire iron and wood construction inward two or three inches. "All the crews of the after guns were knocked over by the concussion, and bled from the nose or ears. Another shot at the same place would have penetrated."

With the two vessels once more in contact, Jones determined to board and capture *Monitor*. Gunners and armorers took up sledgehammers, wedges, crowbars, bits of chain, spikes, and bolts to be jammed into the turret base and stop its motion. Others grabbed flasks of turpentine or balls of oakum saturated with turpentine along with slow matches and torches. Flaming materials would be forced through the top grating of the turret, suffocating the crew or setting the ship on fire and blowing her up.

Peacoats would be thrown over the pilothouse to blind it; grenades were ready to toss down the stacks. The boatswain's gang manned heavy hawsers and chain cables to lash the vessels together. They all grabbed pistols, boarding pikes, and well-sharpened cutlasses. The boatswain piped "boarders away, and Rebels scrambled through the gun ports."

Worden was ready. Ordering the Dahlgrens double shot with canister, he sheared *Monitor* away before boarders jumped across. *Monitor* just missed *Virginia's* submerged stern—by not more than two feet, according to Worden—almost snapping off the foe's rudder and propeller. "Both. . .could have been easily disabled," recalled Jones. He ordered his gunners to concentrate on *Monitor's* pilothouse.

Engineer Stimers considered the pilothouse their only vulnerable spot. It was a box of wrought iron beams, each 12 inches high by 9 inches thick, bolted through the deck and covered by a 2-inch iron plate.

Captain, pilot, and helmsman stood on the grated platform below, chests and heads in a space less than 4 feet wide by 3 feet deep by 4 feet high. The steering wheel or helm was secured to one of the front beams. Worden: "The pilot-house. . .is a foursquare mass of iron, provided with no means of deflecting a ball. I expected trouble from it, and I was not disappointed."

Lieutenant Wood aimed *Virginia's* after pivot gun and—from about 20 yards—delivered a 68-pound explosive shell against the pilothouse at a 30-degree angle. Captain Worden peered through the narrow viewing slit watching for the effect of *Monitor's* shot. The explosion cracked and almost broke the second iron beam, pushed it inward ¾ of an inch, and lifted the top plate, flooding the box with light. It was 11:30 a.m.

Pilot and helmsman were shaken but not injured while a stunned and partially blinded Worden feared serious damage. He ordered the helm to starboard, turning *Monitor* away from the action into shallow water where *Virginia* could not follow and her guns could not reach.

Paymaster Keeler stood below the platform awaiting orders. "[The explosion] was unusually heavy, a flash of

***Monitor* officers on deck in July 1862 include Lt. Samuel Greene (back row, third from left), Paymaster William Keeler (seated middle row second from left), and Surgeon Daniel Logue (seated front right).**
(nhhc)

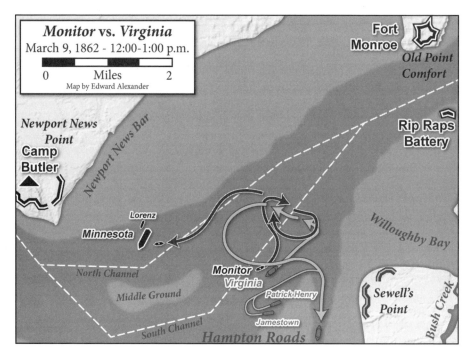

Monitor vs. *Virginia*
March 9, 1862 - 12:00-1:00 p.m.

0   Miles   2
Map by Edward Alexander

Fort Monroe

Old Point Comfort

Newport News Point
Camp Butler

Newport News Bar

Rip Raps Battery

Lorenz
Minnesota

North Channel

Willoughby Bay

Middle Ground

Monitor
Virginia

Patrick Henry

Sewell's Point

Bush Creek

South Channel

Jamestown

Hampton Roads

Monitor vs. *Virginia* 4— The ironclads continue to pound each other while *Virginia* maneuvers to ram or board *Monitor* without success until she plants a shell on *Monitor*'s pilothouse. The contestants part and return to their respective anchorages.

light & a cloud of smoke filled the house. I noticed the Capt. stagger & put his hands to his eyes. . . . The blood was running from his face, which was blackened with the powder smoke." Worden to his officers: "Gentlemen I leave it with you, do what you think best. I cannot see, but do not mind me. Save the *Minnesota* if you can."

Lieutenant Greene came forward, leaving Engineer Stimers in charge of the turret. "[The captain] was a ghastly sight, with his eyes closed and the blood apparently rushing from every pore in the upper part of his face." Worden ordered Greene to assume command before being led to a sofa in his cabin for treatment by Surgeon Logue.

A worried Captain Van Brunt watched from *Minnesota* as *Monitor* retired toward Fort Monroe, thinking she had exhausted her ammunition or sustained some injury. *Virginia* and consorts could again head his way unimpeded. "I then felt to the fullest extent my condition."

He was still hard aground; he had expended most solid shot, and his people were exhausted. The Rebels could take station astern and repeat her demolition of *Congress*. "But even then, in this extreme dilemma, I determined never to give up the ship. . . ." The captain ordered every preparation to destroy *Minnesota*.

The fight had continued over three hours, noted Acting Captain Jones on *Virginia*. "To us the *Monitor* appeared unharmed." To his surprise, she apparently ran off. *Minnesota* lay unprotected on the port beam about a mile away. But his pilots said the tide was falling. With the risk of going aground again, they could not approach the frigate. And *Virginia* must get across the Elizabeth River bar—three miles distant—soon or remain in the Roads until next morning's high water.

Jones waited a while for *Monitor* to return but then decided to retire to the navy yard for maintenance and repairs. After consultation with the lieutenants, the acting captain would later explain, he thought it best to get a new supply of solid shot, have the ram replaced, the gun port shutters put on, the armor belt extended below water, and damaged guns replaced, "and then renew the engagement with every chance of victory."

From *Minnesota's* deck, Captain Van Brunt observed *Virginia's* change of course, heading toward Craney Island. But he was still stuck. "I determined to lighten the ship by throwing overboard my 8-inch guns, hoisting out provisions, starting water, etc."

Confederates excoriated Jones for his decision to retire. Army Captain Norris wanted *Virginia* to sink *Minnesota* with hot shot: "[She] would undoubtedly have been ablaze in a few moments." But *Cumberland* had shot away the muzzle of *Virginia's* port-side hot shot gun the day before. Thus, Norris concluded, "the United States Frigate *Cumberland* saved the United States Frigate *Minnesota*."

A bit later down in *Virginia's* engine room, Engineer Ramsay was astonished to hear cheering. "Rushing on deck, I found we were passing Craney Island on our way to Norfolk, and were being cheered by the soldiers of the battery." He remembered "feeling as though a wet blanket had been thrown over me."

The captain's reasoning was doubtless good, thought the engineer, but leaving *Minnesota* in enemy hands would be a serious blow to Confederate morale. "As the *Merrimac* passed up the river, trailing the ensign of the *Congress* under the stars and bars, she received a tremendous ovation from the crowds that lined the shores, while hundreds of small boats, gay with flags and bunting, converted our course into a triumphal procession."

Meanwhile, Lieutenant Greene had taken station in *Monitor's* pilothouse, finding only minor damage with steering gear intact. He longed to reengage. "We knew that she could not sink us, and I thought I would keep right on pounding her as long as she would stand it." However, by then *Virginia* was over a mile distant and retreating.

Gustavus Vasa Fox (1821-1883) was a former navy lieutenant with 21 years' service who offered the new president a scheme to relieve the beleaguered Fort Sumter before it capitulated. The expedition failed, but the plan so impressed Lincoln that the position of assistant secretary of the navy was created for him. Fox became Welles's right-hand man, making up for the secretary's lack of naval experience and vigorously directing most operational and personnel affairs. (nhhc)

He had strict orders to act on the defensive to protect *Minnesota*. Another hit on the pilothouse could disable the steering apparatus placing them at the mercy of Rebel batteries on Sewell's Point. It would be a long stern chase in a narrow and unfamiliar channel where torpedoes might be lurking. And their wounded captain needed immediate attention. So, Greene let go a few parting shots and turned toward *Minnesota*. He also would be criticized for this decision by armchair admirals.

Paymaster Keeler: "Our iron hatches were slid back & we sprang out on deck which was strewn with fragments of the fight." *Monitor* was struck 22 times: twice on the pilothouse, 9 on the turret, 8 in the side armor, and 3 on deck. She fired in return 53 rounds, over 3 ½ tons of iron by the paymaster's estimate, of which 13 struck the target.

Keeler was collecting iron splinters as mementoes when, "our foe gave us a shell as a parting fire which shrieked just over our heads & exploded about 100 feet from us...." One of *Monitor*'s gunners touched his hat to him and said calmly, "Paymaster there's some more pieces."

"I confess I looked rather anxiously to see if any more were coming," wrote Keeler. He later handed the souvenirs to visitors, sent some to his family, and presented one to President Lincoln, "with the respects of the officers of the *Monitor*."

A flotilla of steamers and boats from Newport News, Fort Monroe, and the various men-of-war surrounded them, "all eager to learn the extent of our injuries & congratulate us on our victory. They told us of the intense anxiety with [which] the conflict was witnessed by thousands of spectators . . . [and] their astonishment was no less on learning that though we were somewhat marked we were uninjured & ready to open the fight again."

Assistant Secretary of the Navy Gustavus Fox waited aboard *Minnesota*. "As we ran along side," wrote Lieutenant Greene to his parents, "Secretary Fox hailed us, and told us we had fought the greatest naval battle on record and behaved as gallantly as men could. He saw the whole fight. I felt proud and happy then Mother, and felt fully repaid for all I had suffered."

In Worden's cabin, Surgeon Logue picked minute iron shards and paint chips from the cornea of his eye and applied cold presses. The blast had embedded coarse grains of powder in his face; he had a minor concussion but required no additional treatment.

"Blind and suffering as he was, Worden's fortitude never forsook him," recalled Greene. "He frequently asked from his bed of pain of the progress of affairs, and when told that the *Minnesota* was saved, he said, 'Then I can die happy.'" Future Admiral John Worden did recover with most of the sight in his right eye, but his face was permanently blackened and his left eye destroyed.

Surviving *Cumberland* and *Congress* sailors watching from Newport News Point saw *Virginia* retreat, seemingly crippled. "We soon learned that she was in a sinking condition," wrote Frederick Curtis, "and our joy knew no bounds. All on shore cheered the brave little 'Monitor' until they were hoarse, and many hugged one another for joy to know that the

hated rebel ram was whipped. So closed two of the most anxious and thrilling days of my experience in the war."

Lieutenant Greene: "All my underclothes were perfectly black with smoke and powder and my person was in the same condition. . . . I had been up so long, and been under such a state of excitement, that my nervous system was completely run down.

"Every bone in my body ached, my limbs and joints were so sore that I could not stand. My nerves and muscles twitched as though electric shocks were continually passing through them and my head ached as if it would burst. Some times I thought my brain would come right out over my eye brows. I lay down and tried to sleep—I might as well have tried to fly."

This dramatic poster, "The First Encounter of Iron-Clads," advertises for the McCormick Harvesting Machine Co., ca. 1891, with a composite illustration of both day's battles. The inset upper right touts "Our N94 Steel Mower" and bottom left shows a reaper as "Our Machine of Steel." *Monitor* **was ubiquitous in late-19th century advertising—refrigerators, playing cards, cigarettes, flour, whiskey, you name it.**
(nhhc)

$\mathcal{D}$ifferent $\mathcal{F}$ates, $\mathcal{D}$ifferent $\mathcal{I}$ronclads

AFTERWORD

BY JOHN V. QUARSTEIN

When President Abraham Lincoln arrived at Fort Monroe on May 6, 1862, his two major goals were to capture Norfolk, Virginia, and open the James River for Union naval operations. Accordingly, Lincoln, with the timid assistance of Flag Officer Louis Goldsborough, personally directed naval actions against Sewell's Point Battery and Confederate forts defending the lower James River.

The USS *Monitor* led the assault against Sewell's Point. Flag Officer Josiah Tattnall, who replaced Franklin Buchanan as commander of the Confederate James River defenses, brought the CSS *Virginia* out from the Elizabeth River to attack *Monitor*. However, the Union ironclad avoided engagement and retreated to the protection of Forts Monroe and Wool (formerly the Rip Raps Battery).

Monitor had been ordered to act on the defensive, which angered many of the ironclad's crew. Tattnall continued to steam around Hampton Roads hoping he might induce *Monitor* to fight, while *Monitor* tried unsuccessfully to bait *Virginia* under the guns of Fort Monroe. Finally, Tattnall gave the order to "fire a gun to windward, and take the ship back to her buoy."

The president was disappointed with the navy's failure to reduce Sewell's Point fortifications or to confront the Confederate ironclad. He reviewed the whole affair from Fort Wool and decided to send Maj. Gen. John E. Wool, commander of the Union Department of Virginia, with brigades of Brig. Gen. John K. F. Mansfield and Brig. Gen. Max Weber to land at Ocean View on the Chesapeake Bay side of Norfolk's Willoughby Spit.

As Wool's command marched toward Norfolk on May 10, Confederates abandoned Norfolk and

On the night of December 31, 1862, the USS *Monitor* sank in heavy seas off the coast of Cape Hatteras, North Carolina. Eyewitnesses on the accompanying warship saw the red distress lantern atop *Monitor's* turret wink out at approximately 1:30 a.m. In 1977, a diving expedition discovered this lantern on the sandy ocean floor near the wreck. It was the last visible sign of *Monitor* before she went down and the first artifact brought up, signaling a rebirth of a Civil War icon. (mmp)

Portsmouth, and set the Gosport Navy Yard ablaze. Tattnall was furious. General Benjamin Huger pulled out without notice after assuring the flag officer the Confederate army would remain in Norfolk for at least another week. *Virginia* was without a port, isolated, and surrounded by Federals.

Tattnall had few options. He could attack the Union fleet, perhaps destroying or damaging several enemy vessels before being enveloped and pounded into submission, or he could try to steam *Virginia* through open ocean to another Southern port like Savannah. The flag officer rejected these alternatives and decided to take his big warship up the James River to defend Richmond.

At 1:00 a.m. on May 11, the pilots advised Tattnall that *Virginia's* draft must be reduced to 18 feet to get over Harrison's Bar at the river mouth. Lieutenant John Taylor Wood noted how the crew sprang into action, removing ballast and everything else but powder and shot. But this was not enough, announced the pilots; with a westerly wind blowing, the ship still could not go as far as the Jamestown flats.

William N. Jeffers, Lt. USN, relieved the wounded Worden after the engagement. The crew missed Worden and sent a letter asking him to return. (nhhc)

Virginia now rode higher in the water, exposing the vulnerable wooden hull. She was no longer an ironclad; she could not engage the Federal fleet. Tattnall had no choice but to run the ship aground off Craney Island and destroy her. While the crew rowed ashore over the next three hours, ten men, including Lt. Catesby Jones, Lt. John Taylor Wood, and Gunner Charles Oliver spread combustibles throughout.

Jones set the slow match and rowed for shore, "by the light of our burning ship." Assistant Engineer E. A. Jack noted as they reached Craney Island: "Flames issuing from the port holes, through the gratings and smokestack - the conflagration was a sight ever to be remembered." "Still unconquered we hauled down our dropping colors [and]. . .with mingled pride and grief, gave her to the flames," recalled Chief Engineer Ashton Ramsay.

It was a beautiful Sunday dawn, May 11, 1862. Suddenly, a huge red and black mass heaved itself skyward over the river, transmitting a blast so terrific that it rattled windows eight miles away. As the crew trudged toward Suffolk, "that last, deep, low, sullen mournful boom told our people, now far away on the march, that their gallant ship was no more." It was, as Landsman Richard Curtis reflected, "a sad finish for such a bright beginning."

Virginia's crew arrived in Suffolk by late afternoon. While they prepared to entrain for Richmond, Landsman Higgins recalled that the ladies of Suffolk "prepared for us bountiful tables on both sides of the street, and dispensed gracious and patriotic hospitality to the tired and hungry men, accompanied with words of cheer for their hearts, made sad by the loss of their gallant vessel."

Lieutenant Jones and the *Virginia* crew were ordered to Fort Darling on Drewry's Bluff looming over a sharp bend in the James River eight miles below Richmond, the only obstacle protecting the Confederate capital from a river approach. Rebel sailors and marines sought revenge by emplacing and manning five naval guns, some salvaged from *Virginia*, alongside army artillery pieces.

On the morning of May 15, five Union warships, including ironclads USS *Monitor* and *Galena*, steamed up the James to test the defenses. River obstructions blocked their advance and forced them to trade salvos with the batteries high on the bluff.

Monitor was unable to elevate its guns to strike the Rebel positions and was hit three times but not seriously damaged. Plunging fire riddled the lightly armored *Galena* causing many casualties. After almost four hours, Union ships retreated downriver. Lieutenant Wood was on the bank with a group of Rebel skirmishers and sharpshooters when *Monitor* glided past. He shouted at the pilothouse, "Tell Captain Jeffers that is not the way to Richmond!"

The Union navy now controlled Hampton Roads, but near Craney Island, the wreck of *Virginia* presented a hazard to navigation. The Union commandant of the Gosport Navy Yard reported in late 1862 that portions of the ironclad's casemate, some weighing as much as 30 tons, had been blown into the main shipping channel.

The navy issued a salvage contract on October 25, 1864, to completely remove remnants of CSS *Virginia* and USS *Congress* and clear the channel. The firm of Underdown & Company raised and processed some scrap but did not fulfill the agreement. Several other contracts during the late 1860s and early 1870s also did not complete the work. Finally, in June 1876, Capt. William West recovered what was left, including two cannons, raised *Virginia's* hulk and towed it to Dry Dock #1 in the Gosport Navy Yard for scrapping.

Most material was sold; however, a few iron plates, as well as the anchor, ship's wheel, and ship's bell, were acquired by museums. Many organizations marketed canes made from the hull's live oak. The Old Dominion Iron and Nail Works produced several tokens looking like small horseshoes affixed to a card stating, "Made from The Armour Plate of The Merrimac—The First

Ironclad 1862." Southerners cherished CSS *Virginia* souvenirs, treating them as holy relics.

Monitor's crew also collected mementos. Paymaster William Keeler gathered shell fragments found around the deck after the battle and sent the end of an exploded shell to President Lincoln, "with the respects of the officers of the *Monitor*." Later, *Monitor* steamed up the Elizabeth River, stopping to recover souvenirs from blackened remains.

Following the defeat at Drewry's Bluff, *Monitor* served in the James River, supporting Maj. Gen. George B. McClellan's Peninsula Campaign. The ironclad needed

repairs, but Flag Officer Goldsborough feared that the new Rebel ironclad CSS *Richmond*, often called *Merrimack II* by Federals, would descend the James from the capital and attack the Union fleet. William Keeler was sick of hearing these rumors: "Some of us will die off one of these days with *MERRIMAC*-ON THE BRAIN."

It was a monotonous summer for the *Monitor* crew. While the ship was stationed near Harrison's Landing, Virginia, interior temperatures hovered near 100 degrees throughout the ship, including a recorded 140 degrees in the galley. Belowdecks, the men "suffered terribly for the want of fresh air." The humidity was so oppressive at night that many braved mosquitoes to sleep on deck.

Commander John Rogers's gunboat flotilla led by *Monitor* and *Galena* approaches Fort Darling on Drewry's Bluff. Sunken hulks block the channel upriver. The city of Richmond appears in the distance. (nhhc)

Monitor also experienced a series of command changes. The first new captain, Lt. William Jeffers, was disliked by the crew. Jeffers was replaced by Commander Thomas Stevens, an intemperate man, and he was succeeded by Commander John Pyne Bankhead.

Bankhead took *Monitor* up to the Washington Navy Yard in Washington D. C. for repairs and improvements. Workers scraped the bottom clean, installed boat davits, cranes, and telescoping funnels, and applied iron patches over shot and shell damage. The little ship became a premier tourist attraction, visited daily by curiosity seekers who often left with souvenirs. In November 1862, Bankhead steamed *Monitor* back down to Hampton Roads to await instructions.

Monitor's Christmas Day orders detailed the ironclad to Beaufort, North Carolina, joining several new *Passaic*-class monitors for a joint army-navy expedition against Wilmington, North Carolina. News of the impending voyage down the coast was not well received by officers or enlisted men, particularly those who had experienced the harrowing trip from New York back in March.

Lieutenant Samuel Dana Greene once again warned, "I do not consider this steamer a seagoing vessel." New crew members heard stories of *Monitor's* last sea cruise, prompting Landsman Jacob Nicklis to write his father, "They say we will have a pretty rough time going around Hatteras, but I hope that it will not be the case."

Captain Bankhead prepared his ship for sea. The ship's surgeon, Dr. Grenville Weeks, noted: the "turret and sight holes were caulked and every possible entrance for water made secure, only the smallest opening was left in the turret top." Seaman George Geer helped secure the hatches with lead putty and prepared rubber gaskets for the portholes as they made "everything about the ship in the way of an opening water tight." Following Navy Department instructions, Bankhead had the turret lifted out of its brass ring and oakum packed around its base.

The side-wheeler USS *Rhode Island*, captained by Commander Stephen Decatur Trenchard, was to tow *Monitor*. If help was needed during the voyage, Bankhead informed Trenchard, a red lantern would be displayed next to the ironclad's white running light on a staff atop the turret. Foul weather delayed the expedition, but Keeler thought this was a good omen, noting that *Monitor* should enjoy the calm following the storm for the trip.

Rhode Island and *Monitor* departed Hampton Roads at 2:30 p.m., December 29, 1862. The voyage passed uneventfully until the next afternoon as wind increased and the sea turned turbulent. When the officers sat down to dinner that evening, remembered Keeler, "everyone [was] cheerful and happy & though the sea was rolling and foaming over our heads the laugh & jest passed 'freely 'round; all rejoicing that at last our monotonous, inactive life had ended & the 'gallant little *Monitor*' would soon add fresh laurels to her name."

Then a series of fierce squalls hit. The ironclad was in "heavy weather, riding one huge wave, plunging through the next, as if shooting straight for the bottom of the ocean." Landsman Francis Butts described the ironclad dropping into a wave "with such force that her hull would tremble."

The pounding sea began to leak into the engine room. Bankhead ordered the bilge pumps started, but nothing held back the flow, which by 9:00 p.m. had risen over a foot deep. The captain put the crew on hand pumps and organized a bucket brigade, which had little effect but to temporarily reduce panic.

John Pyne Bankhead, Commander USN (1821–1867), came from a prominent extended family of Virginia and South Carolina, which included his cousin, Confederate Maj. Gen. John Bankhead Magruder. As captain of *Monitor*, Bankhead would be the last to leave the ship as it was sinking. (nhhc)

"Our little craft struggled long and well," wrote Keeler. "Now her bow would rise on a huge billow and before she could sink into the intervening hollow, the succeeding wave would strike over vessel under her heavy armor with a report like thunder and violence that threatened to tear apart her thin sheet iron bottom and the heavy armor which it supported."

The flood extinguished the boiler fires, rendering *Monitor* helpless. She was "isolated in a sea of hissing seething foam." Bankhead ordered the red lantern displayed and tried to signal *Rhode Island* for assistance. He had the tow lines cut and the anchor dropped to dampen pitching. They launched signal flares. *Rhode Island* still did not notice *Monitor's* distress.

"Words cannot depict the agony of those moments as our little company gathered on top of the turret, stood with a mass of sinking iron beneath them, gazing through the dim light, over the raging waters and an anxiety amounting almost to agony for some evidence of succor from the only source to which we could look for relief," Francis Butts recalled. The "clouds now began to separate, a moon of about half-size beamed out upon the sea, and the *Rhode Island*, now a mile away, became visible. Signals were exchanged, and I felt that the *Monitor* would be saved. . . ."

As *Rhode Island* backed toward *Monitor*, the loose towline fouled the port paddle wheel, causing the side-wheeler to lose control and almost collide with the sinking ironclad. *Rhode Island's* men worked frantically to stabilize the steamer. They launched lifeboats to retrieve *Monitor's* crew. Surging waves carried several sailors overboard as they strove to leap aboard pitching boats alongside the plunging wet deck. Others refused to make the attempt, deciding to take their chances aboard.

"It was half past twelve, the night of 31 December 1862," recalled Landsman Butts, "when I stood on the forecastle of the *Rhode Island*, watching the red and white lights that hung from the pennant staff above the turret, and which now and then were seen as we would perhaps both rise on the sea together, until at last, just as the moon had passed below the horizon, they were lost, and the *Monitor* . . . was seen no more." Four officers and 12 crewmen were lost when she sank in 235 feet of water, 15 miles south of Cape Hatteras, North Carolina.

Neither the USS *Monitor* nor CSS *Virginia* survived the year 1862, but they left a tremendous legacy. The March 8-9 battles of Hampton Roads are among history's most critical naval engagements, but who won? Tactically, the ironclad engagement is considered a draw. Neither vessel was seriously damaged; both remained operational with a few repairs.

Virginia was lionized by her countrymen. In the short term, the Rebel ironclad achieved notable strategic objectives. She devastated the Federal fleet, sinking two capital warships, seriously damaging one, and slightly injuring another. She destroyed three transports and one tug, captured another transport, and badly damaged another tug. She inflicted almost 300 casualties while suffering about 20. It was the greatest United States naval defeat until Pearl Harbor 80 years later.

Virginia dominated Hampton Roads for weeks, blocking Union naval operations toward Norfolk, Portsmouth, and Richmond, and hampering waterborne support of McClellan's operations on the Peninsula. To what degree *Virginia* deterred McClellan is open to speculation, but she certainly had a negative impact on his campaign to capture the Confederate capital. Brigadier General John G. Barnard, chief engineer of the Army of the Potomac, lamented that "the *Merrimack*. . . . proved so disastrous to our subsequent operations."

This *Harper's Weekly* engraving (1863) depicts the USS *Monitor* sinking. Boats from the towing vessel USS *Rhode Island* rescue *Monitor* crewmen from the doomed ironclad. (nhhc)

Union leaders believed *Monitor* was the superior warship, but feared she could be disabled in the next engagement. Flag Officer Goldsborough declared that *Monitor* was to remain in a defensive posture anchored near Fort Wool. He refused to support McClellan's operations against Confederate batteries guarding the York River. *Virginia's* local dominance ended when she was outflanked by land and destroyed by her own men.

Northerners hailed *Monitor* as the victor. She stalemated *Virginia*, prevented *Minnesota's* destruction, and preserved remaining Union warships and transports in Hampton Roads. She relieved Federal fears of a broken blockade and prevented possible attacks on Northern ports.

Regardless of who won, the men of the USS *Monitor* and CSS *Virginia* could proudly claim, "I fought in Hampton Roads." This sentiment was, according to Confederate Army Capt. William Norris, "open sesame to the hearts and minds of our own countrymen. Ah! The thrilling memories of those halcyon days."

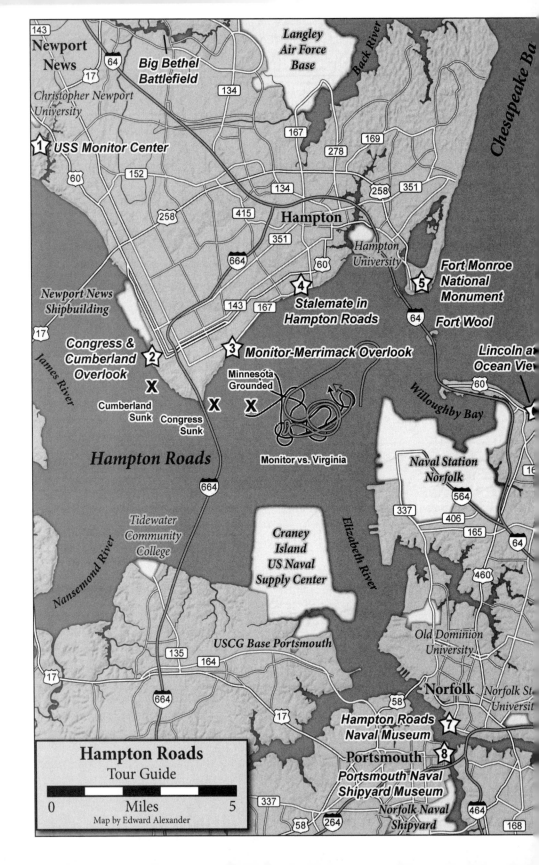

Touring the Battle Site

APPENDIX A

The tour proceeds generally west to east in convenient driving sequence, but stops can be enjoyed in any order.

Stop 1 – The USS Monitor Center at the Mariners' Museum and Park

100 Museum Drive Newport News, VA 23606.

The *Monitor* Collection contains over 200 tons of priceless artifacts recovered from the iconic Civil War ironclad and conserved in a state-of-the-art facility with public viewing. The award-winning Ironclad Revolution exhibition melds artifacts, documents, paintings, personal accounts, and partial reconstructions of the USS *Monitor* and the CSS *Virginia*, including life-size models of the *Monitor* turret and the actual turret in its bath of preservatives. The Museum and the Center are truly premier institutions where cutting-edge maritime archeology meets history for unequaled public education and entertainment. Don't miss it. See Appendix C and https://www.monitorcenter.org/.

Stop 2 – Victory Arch/Victory Landing Park

West Avenue and 25th Street, Newport News, VA 23607.

This city park on Newport News Point is near the former site of Union batteries at Camp Butler and overlooks the anchorage where the USS *Cumberland* and USS *Congress* were attacked by the CSS *Virginia*. It provides excellent views of the Newport News Shipyard, usually with an aircraft carrier or two under repair. The Victory Arch memorializes returning WWI troops. Park on West Avenue near the Victory Arch and walk a block to the waterfront.

Stop 3 – Monitor-Merrimac Overlook Park

1598 16th Street, Newport News, VA 23607.

This tucked away gem provides a wonderful view of the *Monitor-Virginia* battle site with the Monitor-Merrimac Memorial Bridge-Tunnel, Naval Station Norfolk, and Norfolk International Terminals across the waters. The city park includes historical markers, a small beach area, picnic tables, and a dock with great photo ops, especially at sunrise and sunset. Open seven days a week from sunrise to sunset. Free parking.

Stop 4 – Chesapeake Avenue

Driving northeast from Monitor-Merrimac Overlook Park on Chesapeake Avenue along the waterfront affords a continuing view of the 1862 stalemate in Hampton Roads. Park on an adjoining street and walk across to any of several overlooks.

Stop 5 – Fort Monroe Casemate Museum

Building 83, 20 Ingalls Road, Fort Monroe, VA 23651.

This mighty fortress remained a Union bastion near the heart of the Confederacy. Here General Benjamin Butler refused to return escaped slaves, designating them "contraband of war," Gen. George McClellan launched his Peninsula Campaign, and President Abraham Lincoln visited (see next item). The ramparts afford a panoramic view of Hampton Roads and the Chesapeake Bay with all its maritime traffic. You can stand where a young Union soldier watched the USS *Monitor* approach through the dusk while the USS *Congress* blazed. Facilities include a walking tour of the fort, beaches, picnic areas, restaurants, RV park, fishing pier, and 400 years of history. See https://fortmonroe.org/.

Stop 6 – Ocean View Fishing Pier and Restaurant

400 W. Ocean View Avenue, Norfolk, VA 23503.

Near here in May 1862—shortly after the engagements at Hampton Roads—Union forces conducted an amphibious landing under the command of Abraham Lincoln, commander-in-chief. This is the only occasion that a sitting president directly commanded military units in the field. He studied maps, suggested actions, and issued direct orders to subordinate commanders. Blue ranks recaptured Norfolk and the Portsmouth and Gosport shipyards, forcing Rebels to retreat after destroying the CSS *Virginia*. Enjoy the beach, the seashore, and the restaurant. (Fishing pier and restaurant are closed in winter. See http://www.oceanviewfishingpier.com/.) For an excellent telling of this little-known episode, see *Lincoln Takes Command: The Campaign to Seize Norfolk and the Destruction of the CSS Virginia* by Steve Norder (Savas Beatie, 2020).

Stop 7 – Hampton Roads Naval Museum

1 Waterside Drive, Ste 248, Norfolk, VA 23510.

This museum is operated by the Naval History & Heritage Command to celebrate the long history of the U.S. Navy in the region. Permanent exhibits cover the Battle of the Chesapeake (1781), the Civil War, the Great White Fleet, World War II, and the Cold War. The museum is the official repository of the remains of two Civil War shipwrecks: USS *Cumberland* and CSS *Florida*. It is co-located with Nauticus, an exciting interactive science and technology center exploring the power of the sea. Nauticus also is the home of the Iowa-class battleship USS *Wisconsin* where visitors can tour this most impressive descendant of Civil War ironclads.

https://www.history.navy.mil/content/history/museums/hrnm.html   and https://nauticus.org/

Stop 8 – Portsmouth Naval Shipyard Museum

2 High Street, Portsmouth, VA 23704.

This small museum explores the history of America's oldest and largest naval shipyard, founded in 1767, and burned three times by retreating armies. The yard was known in 1862 as Gosport; it also was referred to as the Norfolk Navy Yard. The CSS *Virginia* was constructed here in the nation's first dry dock, which is still in use. Other historic launchings include America's first battleship, the USS *Texas,* and the world's first aircraft carrier, the USS *Langley.* You will find beautiful ship models, uniforms, military artifacts, and exhibits interpreting eighteenth, nineteenth, and twentieth century life in Portsmouth.

http://www.portsmouthnavalshipyardmuseum.com.

Civil War Ironclads

APPENDIX B

BY JOHN V. QUARSTEIN AND DWIGHT HUGHES

The USS *Monitor* and CSS *Virginia* served as prototypes for massive wartime ironclad building programs. Around the South's harbors, coasts, and rivers, Confederates struggled to construct casemated ironclads like *Virginia*, while in the North, "Monitor mania" produced a flood of new vessels.

The first ironclads, however, were modeled on neither. The strange little ram CSS *Manassas* had been privately converted in New Orleans from a steam towboat and armored with 1.25-inch plate. On October 12, 1861, *Manassas* rammed the USS *Richmond* at the mouth of the Mississippi, causing little damage but losing the iron prow and unseating one engine. With shells bouncing off the sloped iron "turtle back," she fled upriver to join the squadron defending the city.

In May 1861, U.S. Navy Secretary Gideon Welles appointed Commander John Rodgers to establish "a naval armament" on the Mississippi and Ohio rivers and to cooperate with army commanders. Rodgers partnered with James B. Eads, a wealthy St. Louis industrialist and prominent civil engineer, and Samuel Pook, a noted naval architect, to produce the first uniform river warship class.

Named after river cities, the seven "city class" gunboats were shallow-draft, broad-beamed, paddlewheel river ironclads, also known as "Pook Turtles." Despite shortcomings—such as relatively light 2.5-inch armor—they effectively combined firepower, protection, and mobility for this unprecedented form of inland naval warfare.

In February 1862, Flag Officer Andrew Hull Foote teamed with Brig. Gen. U. S. Grant to take Fort Henry on the Tennessee River and Fort Donelson on the Cumberland. The new gunboats pounded poorly constructed Fort Henry into submission before Union troops arrived. At Fort Donelson the ironclads took considerable damage until "Unconditional Surrender" Grant surrounded and battered the Rebels into capitulation.

Confederates abandoned most of middle Tennessee and all of Kentucky. The city-class ironclads became the backbone of the Mississippi River Squadron, taking part in almost every action on the upper Mississippi and its tributaries. They were

The forward section of the city-class ironclad, USS *Cairo*, rests on a barge after being salvaged from Yazoo River near Vicksburg in 1964. During the Yazoo Pass Expedition clearing mines for the attack on Haines Bluff, she became the first ship sunk by a remotely detonated mine, 12 December 1862. *Cairo's* restored remains now rest on display at Vicksburg National Military Park. A wooden framework completes the vessel's outline. (nhhc)

The turtle-backed ironclad ram CSS *Manassas* (right) charges at Farragut's fleet passing the Lower Mississippi forts on the way to New Orleans. The lead ship at left is Farragut's flagship, USS *Hartford*, with a Confederate fire raft burning alongside. (nhhc)

Starting at Forts Henry and Donelson, the city-class ironclad USS *Carondelet* would become a battle-scarred veteran of every major engagement on the Mississippi. She was the first to run the batteries at Island No. 10 (April 1862), and fought at Fort Pillow (April 1862) and the Battle of Memphis (June 1862). *Carondelet* was badly damaged and grounded in an engagement with the ironclad CSS *Arkansas* on the Yazoo River (July 1862). In 1863, Carondelet participated in the Steele's Bayou fiasco as Grant tried to get at Vicksburg, bombarded the city during the siege, ran the batteries, and assisted Grant across the river. Finally, *Carondelet* was part of the ill-fated Red River Expedition in spring 1864. (nhhc)

a major factor in Grant's victory at Vicksburg and in securing the Father of Waters for the Union.

For Confederates, the battle of New Orleans in April 1862 demonstrated the same problems that plagued *Virginia*. Union Flag Officer David G. Farragut's deep-water warships blew past forts at the mouth of the Mississippi and surged upriver to the city where two potentially powerful, but deeply flawed and incomplete Rebel ironclads were undergoing furious final construction.

Confederate naval officers described the CSS *Mississippi* as "the strongest. . .most formidable war vessel that had ever been built." Without trained ship carpenters, this strange behemoth was built with flat planes and square corners like a floating house. She carried four and a half feet of iron and wood armor with twenty guns, and was powered by eight huge boilers, three engines, and three propellers.

Mississippi launched on April 19, 1862, but the Tredegar Iron Works had not delivered the propeller shafts, and guns were not mounted. Farragut arrived five days later. *Mississippi's* crew set the helpless ship afire and fled upriver, a fate shared by many of the South's iron monsters.

The CSS *Louisiana* was just as big, with two paddle wheels in a center-well, one behind the other, two propellers, sixteen guns, and a casemate armored with two layers of railroad iron. The hull was constructed of green wood for lack of seasoned supplies; water poured through crevices inundating the gundeck knee deep. Her engines were not fully operational; the paddle wheels worked but inefficiently.

Louisiana was secured to the bank just above Fort St. Philip as a floating battery. Frustrated crewmen got off only a few rounds as Union warships thundered past. They could not train the guns beyond a small arc or

elevate them over five degrees. Afterwards, the men set fires and she exploded. Although these two huge, heavy vessels were almost impregnable and armed with powerful batteries, they were grossly underpowered and hardly maneuverable in the swift flowing river. The CSS *Manassas* was riddled, forced aground, and burned.

One Rebel ironclad had spectacular, if temporary, success. The CSS *Arkansas* was laid down in Memphis with her sister ship, the CSS *Tennessee*, but in April 1862, Union forces threatened that city. *Tennessee* could not be launched and was burned on the stocks. *Arkansas* moved south to Greenwood City, Mississippi, on the Yazoo River to be completed by Lt. Isaac Newton Brown on the riverbank under summer sun.

Union gunboats advance up the Tennessee River on 6 February 1862 to attack Fort Henry. (nhhc)

On July 15, still only partially plated with railroad T-rails, *Arkansas* descended the Yazoo into the Mississippi, fought with and almost sank the city-class ironclad USS *Carondelet*, and blasted through massed guns of a surprised Federal fleet into Vicksburg to the cheers of the population observing from the bluffs. A few days later, the ironclad USS *Essex* and wooden ram *Star of the West* attacked *Arkansas* at the city dock without causing serious damage. She then went to the defense of Baton Rouge where the engines failed, and the crew scuttled her to avoid capture.

Confederate Naval Constructor John Luke Porter modified the South's ironclad designs for smaller, lighter draft vessels, more appropriate for riverine and harbor defense. Nevertheless, persistent difficulties included poor propulsion systems, construction delays,

limited production of iron and machinery, an overtaxed transportation network, and shortage of skilled workers. The South eventually launched 22 ironclads, but most of them laid down in 1862 would not be in service until 1864.

The CSS *Arkansas* charges through an astonished Union fleet above Vicksburg, July 15, 1862. This engraving was published in *Battles and Leaders of the Civil War* based on a drawing by marine artist J.O. Davidson. (nhhc)

Union ironclad production dramatically increased and evolved. Subsequent classes strove to correct *Monitor* design problems, but still were essentially floating batteries. They required towing from port to port, were

The large twin-turret monitor *Miantonomoh* is moored near the Washington Navy Yard, D.C. ca. 1865 with the smaller monitor *Montauk* tied up alongside (left) and others behind. Masts in the background mark the former Confederate ironclad *Stonewall* before she is sold to Japan. Note large shiphouse at right. (nhhc)

unseaworthy and ineffective as blockaders. They had limited firepower, inadequate gun elevation, and slow volume of fire. A total of 49 ships were produced in several classes, including two-, four-, and six-turreted models.

On January 31, 1863, Confederate ironclads CSS *Chicora* and CSS *Palmetto State* struck at the blockading fleet outside of Charleston, South Carolina, damaging four Union vessels but only temporarily disrupting the blockade before returning to port.

The ill-fated CSS *Atlanta*, converted from the British blockade runner *Fingal*, mounted excellent engines and two powerful Brooke rifles in a deep, 16-foot draft. On June 17, 1863, *Atlanta* forayed into Savannah's Wassau Sound to take on the improved monitors USS *Nahant* and *Weehawken*, but ran aground. The monitors pounded *Atlanta* with their 9- and 15-inch Dahlgrens, penetrated the armor, and forced her surrender. *Atlanta* was repaired and taken into the Union navy.

Monitors, however, did not do well against shore fortifications. Rear Admiral Samuel Francis DuPont attacked Charleston Harbor on April 7, 1863 with seven monitors, the USS *New Ironsides*, and the experimental tower ironclad *Keokuk*. The navy secretary had high expectations for the operation, but DuPont was doubtful.

General P. G. T. Beauregard created in-depth defenses with torpedoes, two ironclads, and forts mounting 77 heavy guns, including Brooke rifles firing armor-piercing bolts. The slow-firing ironclads managed to

Rear Admiral DuPont's monitors unsuccessfully challenge Fort Sumter and take a battering. (loc)

get off only 55 shots while taking over 400 hits. Several monitors were severely damaged, and *Keokuk* sunk. Charleston was never conquered from the water.

By 1864, Confederates launched more effective ironclads. The CSS *Albemarle*, built in a North Carolina cornfield on the banks of the Roanoke River, dominated western Albemarle Sound through summer 1864. In April, she rammed and sank the small paddle steamer, USS *Southfield*. Two weeks later, she repulsed a determined attack by seven wooden gunboats, seriously injuring three but sustaining damage herself. Frustrated Federals finally destroyed *Albemarle* on October 27 when bold navy Lt. William B. Cushing ran right up against her in a steam launch with a spar torpedo.

The former Confederate casemate ironclad CSS *Tennessee* flies the Union flag as the USS *Tennessee* after the Battle of Mobile Bay. (nhhc)

Meanwhile, the powerful ironclad CSS *Tennessee* anchored the Confederate squadron in Mobile Bay, Alabama. On August 5, 1864, David Farragut, now an admiral, again blasted by harbor entrance forts, losing the monitor USS *Tecumseh* to a torpedo. He ganged up on *Tennessee* with his big, seagoing warships and four monitors.

Three sloops-of-war rammed *Tennessee*. New monitors USS *Manhattan* and the double-turreted *Chickasaw* delivered point blank 11- and 15-inch Dahlgren rounds that broke the casemate and began to dismantle the Rebel ironclad, killing several crewmen. *Tennessee* surrendered.

The final ironclad engagement was the battle of Trent's Reach, January 23-24, 1865, a desperate attempt by the Richmond Squadron to destroy the Union supply base at City Point. Federal shore batteries and the twin-turreted USS *Onondaga* blocked the path of ironclads CSS *Richmond*, *Fredericksburg*, and *Virginia II*. Two shots from the monitor's 15-inch Dahlgrens broke *Virginia II* 's shield; the squadron turned back. Confederates destroyed their remaining ironclads in Richmond, Savannah, and Charleston as the nation collapsed.

The CSS *Virginia* epitomized the Confederacy's ironclad program as an attempt to overcome overwhelming enemy resources with superior technology. The USS *Monitor* fathered a fleet of similar vessels that contributed to victory. Their clash at Hampton Roads stimulated the ironclad revolution around the globe.

The USS Monitor Center at The Mariners' Museum and Park

APPENDIX C

WWW.MARINERSMUSEUM.ORG

In 1987, The Mariners' Museum and Park in Newport News, Virginia, competed with several institutions around the United States for the honor of being the repository of artifacts recovered from the wreck site of the American Civil War ironclad USS *Monitor*. The museum, designated as America's National Maritime Museum, has a vast collection consisting of more than 32,000 discrete artifacts, and more than one million items in its library and archives.

The choice to award The Mariners' Museum with *Monitor's* objects changed the institution forever. The partnership with the National Oceanic and Atmospheric Administration (NOAA), though modest at first, became something monumental in 1997 when NOAA published a new preservation plan for the *Monitor* National Marine Sanctuary.

The wreck was deteriorating, due to a combination of natural and manmade phenomena. The decision was made to recover the most significant parts of the wreck, including much of the vessel's engine room, and would culminate in the raising of its iconic revolving gun turret.

After NOAA's plan was approved in 1998, artifacts began being recovered, and by 2000, The Mariners' Museum had crafted a plan of its own to create a state-of-the-art conservation facility, as well as an exhibition to showcase this nationally important story.

The Mariners' Museum and Park's staff did their best to prepare for the onslaught of artifacts arriving from the recovery expeditions, and found imaginative ways to house the materials with a variety of repurposed containers and steel tanks. Since the laboratory facility was still in the planning stages, there was no space large enough to house all the artifact tanks indoors. The majority of large objects resided outside, with a few having only partial cover. With an intent toward an inclusive process, the Museum made every attempt possible to ensure artifact tanks were accessible to public viewing by adding ramps and decking.

The storage situation was not ideal, but a marine archaeological metals conservation project of this type and scale was unprecedented. It was clear the playbook would need to be written as it went along. All the while, artifacts just kept arriving with the focus being finding places to store the materials.

Entrance to the Mariners' Museum & Park, Newport News, Virginia. (mmp)

By the time the turret was recovered in 2002, the press surrounding the turret recovery was unprecedented. Traditional news

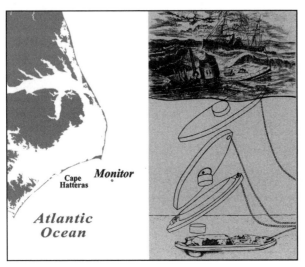

When *Monitor* sank, she flipped upside down. The turret detached and landed with the hull on top. (noaa)

outlets covered the story, to be sure. The expedition was featured on *The Daily Show*, and became part of Jay Leno's monologue on *The Tonight Show*. Clearly, this was a story that transcended traditional interests and had made its way into popular culture – much as the *Monitor* had itself, 140 years before. With the recovery of the turret, the Museum now held more than 210 tons of the ironclad, or nearly one-fifth of the vessel.

Notable early dates in the turret conservation timeline include the removal of the 'spider' lifting assembly in April 2003, exposing the entire interior of the artifact. This allowed the removal of the gun slides, gun carriages, and ultimately, the guns themselves in September 2004.

In 2005, construction began on a permanent conservation facility for the storage and treatment of *Monitor* artifacts. Due to their sheer size and weight, the turret, the propulsion engine, and steam condenser required they be moved into the new lab space prior to the installation of the walls and roof. Aided by multiple teams, the object moves required several stages of planning and execution.

The turret had to be the first artifact moved. Because of the enormous weight of not only the object, but also the approximately 90,000 gallons of water in which it was submerged, a reinforced independent concrete pad had to be constructed prior to the installation of the

The later stages of the long-range preservation plan focused on recovery, conservation, and exhibition of major artifacts along with survey and stabilization of remaining wreckage. (noaa)

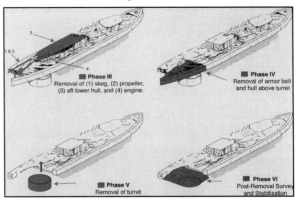

rest of the lab's floor. Once the pad was completed and cured in February 2005, the turret was wrapped with a steam-powered heating system to keep it from freezing. The treatment tank wall was cut free from its base and removed.

The imposing object was then rolled across the property via a multi-joint articulated platform bed to the new concrete pad. The turret was gently lowered onto a new tank base with hydraulic jacks, in a delicate process carried out in conjunction with a rigging team from Lockwood Brothers Incorporated. The original tank wall was then lowered around the turret and welded to the new base by staff from the Newport News Shipbuilding Apprentice School.

The remaining concrete for the laboratory floor was then poured in stages. In May, the engine and condenser were lifted out of their original treatment tank by crane and placed onto a flatbed trailer. The trailer was then driven alongside new artifact treatment tanks. The crane was repositioned, and each object was carefully ensconced into its new treatment tank.

By late 2006, the Batten Conservation Complex was completed and was composed of a large Wet Lab containing the artifact treatment tanks, a workroom area for temporary object storage; and a Clean Lab for final artifact treatment. The new facility was officially opened along with the *Ironclad Revolution* exhibit in 2007 as the USS *Monitor* Center at The Mariners' Museum and Park.

To date, the USS *Monitor* Project is the largest marine archaeological metals conservation project in the world. The USS *Monitor* Center is committed to fully stabilizing every artifact recovered from the ironclad, including the iconic 120-ton revolving gun turret, and personal

Monitor's **turret was raised from the seabed in a custom-built "spider" assembly. The turret is upside down filled with mud, debris, equipment, guns, and crew remains.** (mmp)

After excavating the interior of the inverted turret, lab workers attach straps to lift the guns out. The gun carriages have already been removed. (mmp)

items associated with the crew, such as engraved silverware and clothing. The institution strives to provide a unique, educational, and entertaining experience.

Museum visitors may watch conservators work via a special viewing platform that enables them to see directly into the Wet Lab, experience life aboard ship by walking through re-constructed officers' quarters, design their own ironclad vessels, witness the battle of Hampton Roads, and touch original iron armor from the ship. If a visit is not possible, content about *Monitor* may be found on the Museum's website, as well as a live video stream into the Wet Lab.

The Museum employs an international team of marine archaeological conservators to preserve nearly 5,000 artifacts from NOAA's *Monitor* Collection at the USS *Monitor* Center's Batten Conservation Complex. The American Institute for Conservation (AIC) is a national organization that defines all professional standards for the field of conservation. The conservation team adheres to AIC's "Code of Ethics" and "Guidelines for Practice," while conserving all materials from NOAA's *Monitor* Collection.

Conservators on the project have been so effective in their public advocacy for the conservation project that in 2006, the Museum received the prestigious Keck Award from the International Institute for Conservation (IIC) for "promoting public understanding and appreciation of the accomplishments of the conservation profession."

This view shows the turret interior with armor plates, bolt and rivet heads, and mammoth gun port stoppers (inverted) with large bolts installed to hold them in place. (mmp)

The USS *Monitor* Conservation Project is recognized nationally and internationally for its pioneering conservation work with marine artifacts. Treatment innovations and research regarding USS *Monitor* objects are presented at local, national, and international professional conferences. Presentations by conservation team members are also shared with the public via lectures, social media, and a dedicated blog platform.

Conserving USS *Monitor* is an ongoing, multi-decade commitment. It will take approximately 30 years to fully stabilize every artifact recovered from the ship to enable their display. The USS *Monitor* conservation project is a national public-private partnership of international significance, focused on preserving the technological artifacts and personal stories from an iconic Civil War ironclad.

Monitor's inventor, John Ericsson, came to America from Sweden to participate in the American dream. The ship's officers and crew hailed from northern and southern states as well as Europe. One hundred fifty years ago, Ericsson's vessel and *Monitor's* crew were the manifestation of the nation's industrial might, and the notion of the United States of America as a melting pot. Today, The Mariners' Museum and Park is honored to continue to preserve this National Historical Landmark and its stories for future generations.

The state-of-the-art Batten Conservation Laboratory opened in 2007. It houses thousands of small and large Monitor artifacts and allows scientists to study the corrosion process while cleaning and preserving them. In this Wet Lab, the foreground preservation tank contains the steam engine; the larger tank holds the turret. Visitors can view tanks and activities from a catwalk through windows at left. (mmp)

BATTLE OF HAMPTON ROADS

UNITED STATES NORTH ATLANTIC BLOCKADING SQUADRON

Flag Officer (Capt.) Louis Malesherbes Goldsborough (absent from Hampton Roads on March 8-9, 1862)

Capt. John Marston (Acting commander of U. S. Navy vessels in Hampton Roads on March 8-9, 1862)

USS *Roanoke*, *Merrimack*-class screw frigate, 674 men, 43 guns
Capt. John Marston

USS *Minnesota*, *Merrimack*-class screw frigate, 646 men, 43 guns
Capt. Gershom Jaques Van Brunt

USS *Congress*, sailing frigate, 480 men, 52 guns
Lt. Joseph B. Smith
Lt. Austin Pendergrast (executive officer and acting captain upon Smith's death)

USS *St. Lawrence*, sailing frigate, 480 men, 52 guns
Capt. Hugh Young Purviance

USS *Cumberland*, sailing sloop-of-war, 400 men, 24 guns
Commander William Radford (absent from the ship on March 8, 1862)
Lt. George Upham Morris (executive officer and acting captain on March 8, 1862)

USS *Monitor*, ironclad steam battery, 49 men, 2 guns
Lt. John Lorimer Worden
Lt. Samuel Dana Greene (executive officer and acting captain upon Worden's wounding)
Chief Engineer Alban C. Stimers (Navy Department observer)

USS *Dragon*, steam gunboat, 42 men, 2 guns
Acting Master W. Watson

USS *Zouave*, steam tug, approx. 20 men, 2 guns
Acting Master Henry Reaney

U. S. ARMY DEPARTMENT OF VIRGINIA
Maj. Gen. John Ellis Wool

Union Camp Butler on Newport News Point
Brig. Gen. Joseph King Fenno Mansfield

CONFEDERATE STATES NAVAL UNITS IN HAMPTON ROADS

Flag Officer (Capt.) Franklin Buchanan. Flagship: CSS *Virginia*
Lt. Robert Dabney Minor, Flag Lieutenant

CSS *Virginia*, casemate ironclad, 320 men, 10 guns
No commanding officer assigned.
Lt. Catesby ap Roger Jones (executive officer and acting captain upon
Buchanan's wounding)
Chief Engineer Henry Aston Ramsay

CSS *Beaufort*, propeller steam gunboat, 35 men, 1 gun
Lt. William Harwar Parker

CSS *Raleigh*, propeller steam gunboat, 35 men, 1 gun
Lt. Joseph W. Alexander

JAMES RIVER SQUADRON
Commander John Randolph Tucker

CSS *Patrick Henry*, sidewheel gunboat, 150 men, 12 guns
Commander John Randolph Tucker

CSS *Jamestown*, sidewheel gunboat, 150 men, 2 guns
Lt. Joseph Nicholson Barney

CSS *Teaser*, steam tug, 25 men, 1 gun
Lt. William A. Webb

CONFEDERATE ARMY OF THE PENINSULA
Maj. Gen. John Bankhead Magruder

CONFEDERATE DEPARTMENT OF NORFOLK
Maj. Gen. Benjamin Huger

Suggested Reading

"Our Little Monitor:" The Greatest Invention of the Civil War
Anna Gibson Holloway and Jonathan W. White
The Kent State University Press (2018)
ISBN 978-1-60635-314-1

Part 1 narrates *Monitor's* story from inception through her loss off Cape Hatteras. The political and technological dimensions of the ironclad's development are well presented along with an excellent overview of the Battle of Hampton Roads followed by a discussion of the battle's aftermath and the frustrating later careers of both *Monitor* and the CSS *Virginia*. Included is a unique discourse on the vessel's impact for nineteenth century (and since) popular culture or "*Monitor* mania." Finally, Part 1 describes the search for and partial recovery of the little ironclad in the late 1990s and early 2000s. Part 2 reproduces previously unpublished letters and journal entries. "Our Little *Monitor*" combines thorough research, new information, a fresh perspective, and cutting-edge maritime archaeology with plentiful illustrations and numerous first-person quotes.

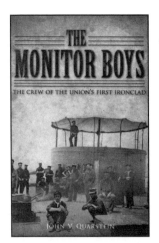

The Monitor Boys: The Crew of the Union's First Ironclad
John V. Quarstein
The History Press (2011)
ISBN 978-1-59629-455-4

Historian John Quarstein compiled numerous bits of scattered historical data providing the first comprehensive picture of Americans serving in a revolutionary ironclad warship. They called themselves "The Monitor Boys." They were agents of change in naval warfare, suffering storms, battles, boredom, and disaster with uncommon fortitude. Included are a detailed chronology, and appendices with crewmen biographies, casualties and statistics, and ship dimensions. These men risked everything in the celebrated "cheesebox on a raft" and became the hope of a nation wracked by war.

The CSS Virginia: Sink Before Surrender
John V. Quarstein
The History Press (2012)
ISBN 978-1-60949-580-0

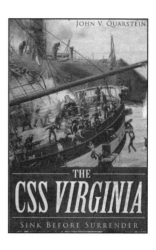

Virginia was the epitome of Confederate naval strategy and execution—the brainchild of innovative, dedicated, and professional men, but the victim of poor planning and coordination, hurried construction without testing or refinement, and a dearth of critical resources. Still, she was perceived as an existential threat to the Union. This is the compelling story of an ironclad underdog, with detailed appendices, crew member biographies, and a complete chronology of ship and crew.

The Battle of Hampton Roads: New Perspectives on the USS Monitor and the CSS Virginia
Harold Holzer and Tim Mulligan, editors
Fordham University Press (2006)
ISBN 0-8232-2480-5 (hardcover), ISBN 0-8232-2481-3 (pbk.)

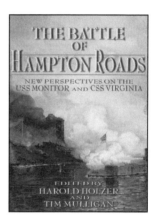

Ten original essays, written by leading historians, explore every aspect of the historic battle—from construction of and life aboard these "iron coffins" to tactics, strategy, and debates about who really won. Co-published with The Mariners' Museum, home to the USS *Monitor* Center, this is an authoritative guide to military, political, technological, and cultural dimensions of the engagement. It includes a portfolio of classic lithographs, drawings, and paintings.

Iron Coffin: War, Technology and Experience aboard the USS Monitor, Updated Edition
David A. Mindell
The Johns Hopkins University Press (2000, 2012)
ISBN 978-1-4214-0520-9

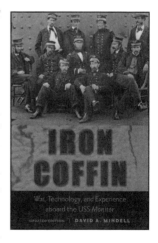

This is an account of ironclad warships and the human dimension of modern warfare. Mindell explores how mariners—fighting "blindly" below the waterline—lived in and coped with the metal monster they called the "iron coffin." New ironclad technology changed not only the tools but also the experience of combat, anticipating mechanized, pushbutton warfare. The compelling letters of Paymaster William F. Keeler and his shipmates help recreate the thrills and dangers of living and fighting aboard *Monitor*.

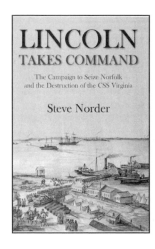

Lincoln Takes Command: The Campaign to Seize Norfolk and the Destruction of the CSS Virginia
Steve Norder
Savas Beatie (2020)
ISBN 978-1-61121-457-4

In May 1862—shortly after the engagements at Hampton Roads—Union forces conducted an amphibious landing under the command of Abraham Lincoln, commander-in-chief. This was the only occasion that a sitting president directly commanded military units in the field. Blue ranks recaptured Norfolk along with the Portsmouth and Gosport shipyards, forcing Rebels to retreat after destroying the CSS *Virginia*. See Appendix A, tour stop 6.

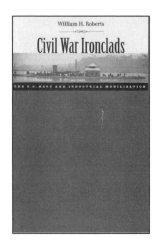

Civil War Ironclads: The U. S. Navy and Industrial Mobilization
William H. Roberts
The Johns Hopkins University Press (2002)
ISBN 978-0-8018-8751-2

This is the first comprehensive study of U. S. wartime ironclad construction starting with the USS *Monitor*. The navy faced enormous engineering challenges with an experimental technology in a huge and immensely complex acquisition program. An unprecedented and nearly independent "project office" produced around 50 *Monitor*-class warships, but suffered constant design changes, technical blunders, cost overruns, delays, and capital starvation, leading to financial ruin for most of the builders. Contrary to belief, Roberts concludes, the ironclad program set navy shipbuilding back a generation.

Aboard the USS Monitor: 1862: The Letters of Acting Paymaster William Frederick Keeler, U. S. Navy To his Wife, Anna
Robert W. Daly, editor
United States Naval Institute (1964)
ASIN B000CFUS9Q

William Frederick Keeler's regular letters to his loving wife Anna provide the most detailed and thoughtful first-person account of the difficult life and dramatic events in *Monitor*. He was an insightful observer and active participant with an engaging writing style that places the reader in the action. Keeler's technically savvy descriptions fill in details of other documentation including those of John Ericsson, navy officials, and other crewmembers. Not in print, but available used.

Iron Afloat: The Story of the Confederate Armorclads
William N. Still, Jr.
Vanderbilt University Press (1971)
ISBN 0-8265-1161-9

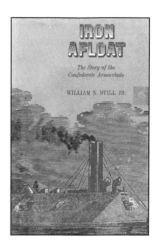

When the Civil War began, the South had virtually no navy, few seamen, and limited shipbuilding facilities. To defend its ports against a well-established Northern navy, the South resorted to innovation and the Confederate ironclad navy was born. The government commissioned and put into operation 22 armorclad vessels of war. This is their story from program inception, through myriad construction difficulties, their dramatic careers (including gripping battle descriptions), to eventual destruction or surrender.

The Introduction of the Ironclad Warship (Classics of Naval Literature)
James Phinney Baxter, 3rd
Naval Institute Press (reprint 2000)
ISBN 978-1-5575-0218-6

This landmark study, originally published in 1933, was the first comprehensive history covering the ascendance of the ironclads and it remains the standard text. Notable ships discussed are the USS *Princeton*, USS *Monitor*, USS *Merrimack*, HMS *Warrior*, HMS *Achilles*, and the CSS *Virginia*. From U. S. and British sources, the author relates the development of these unique vessels, including revolutions in naval ordnance, propulsion technology, and ship construction.

Clad in Iron: The American Civil War and the Challenge of British Naval Power
Howard J. Fuller
Naval Institute Press (2008)
ISBN 978-1-59114-297-3

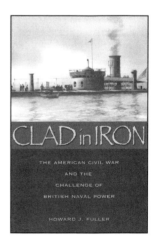

British intervention in the Civil War backed up by the Royal Navy posed a more dangerous long-range threat to the Union than did the Confederate States Navy, including the CSS *Virginia*. The first Union ironclads—the USS *Monitor*, USS *New Ironsides*, and USS *Galena*—were constructed not just to counter a temporary rebellion, but also, and perhaps primarily, to deter the growing British and French seagoing ironclads potentially threatening Northern coasts, ports, and commerce. They had more success in the critical role of discouraging British meddling than fighting Rebels. This work corrects common misconceptions by placing the ironclad revolution in its international strategic, diplomatic, and technological context.

About the Author

Dwight Hughes is a public historian, author, and speaker in Civil War naval history. Dwight graduated from the U. S. Naval Academy in 1967 with a major in History and Government. He served 20 years as a Navy surface warfare officer on most of the world's oceans in ships ranging from destroyer to aircraft carrier and with river forces in Vietnam.

Lieutenant Commander Hughes taught Naval ROTC at the University of Rochester, earning an MA in Political Science. He later earned an MS in Information Systems Management from USC. In his final sea tour, Commander Hughes planned and conducted convoy exercises with over 20 ships of the Maritime Prepositioned Force, Diego Garcia, Indian Ocean.

Dwight's second career was software engineering, primarily in geographic feature naming data and electronic mapping under contract for the U. S. Geological Survey. A ridge in Antarctica is named after him in recognition of contributions to Antarctic databases and information services.

Dwight is author of *A Confederate Biography: The Cruise of the CSS Shenandoah* (Naval Institute Press, 2015) and a contributing author at the Emerging Civil War blog. He has presented at numerous Civil War roundtables, historical conferences, and other venues. See his website: https://civilwarnavyhistory.com.

EMERGING CIVIL WAR SERIES